Filming the Fantastic with Virtual Technology

This book brings fantasy storytelling to a whole new level by providing an in-depth insight into the tools used for virtual reality, augmented reality, and motion capture in order to repurpose them to create a virtual studio for filmmaking. Added to the tools above is 360 cinema. We would define 360 cinema as, in our opinion, referring to an event captured in 360 degrees where the audience can choose the viewpoint. Gone are the long days and months of post before seeing your final product. Composites and CG characters in computer graphics can now be shot together as fast as a live-action show.

Using off-the-shelf software and tools, authors Mark Sawicki and Juniko Moody document the set-up and production pipelines of the modern virtual/motion-capture (mocap) studio. They reveal the procedures and secrets for making movies in virtual sets. The high-end technology that enabled the creation of films such as The Lord of the Rings (2001–2003), *Avatar* (2009), and *The Jungle Book* (2016) is now accessible for smaller, independent production companies. Do you want your actors to perform inside of an Unreal® Game Engine set and interact with the environment? Do you want to be able to put your live-action camera on a jib or dolly, and move effortlessly through both a live-action and a virtual space together? Do you want live performers interacting with giants, elves, and other creatures manipulated by motion capture in real time? This book discusses all of these scenarios and more, showing readers how to create high-quality virtual content using alternative, cost-effective technology.

Tutorials, case studies, and project breakdowns provide essential tips on how to avoid and overcome common pitfalls, making this book an indispensable guide for both beginners to create virtual backlot content and more advanced VFX users wanting to adopt best practices when planning and directing virtual productions with Reality™ software and performance capture equipment such as Qualysis.

Mark Sawicki entered the visual effects field as an effects cameraman, animator, and compositor in the late 70s. As a co-supervisor for Area 51 on Tom Hanks special "From the Earth to the Moon" (1998), Sawicki was part of the combined use of models, motion control, and computer graphics imagery (CGI) as a pivotal transition point between the traditional and digital eras. Mark went on to become visual effects supervisor and lead cameraman for Custom Film effects working on such films as Christopher Nolan's *The Dark Knight Rises* (2012). At the start of the 21st century, Mark took a hiatus from production to write books, create video programs for the Stan Winston School of Character Arts, and to teach at a variety of film schools. He has now re-entered the field as a virtual production artist and corporate trainer.

Juniko Moody graduated from University of Southern California (USC) Cinema and entered the industry as a motion control and compositing technician working for New World Studios, Ultimatte Corporation, and Industrial Light and Magic (ILM). She entered the digital field working for Eastman Kodak's Cineon project digitally restoring the Disney classic *Snow White* (originally released 1937, restored 1993) and went on to work for Warner Digital and Sony Imageworks as a digital artist. She was hired by Walt Disney Feature Animation to provide CGI lighting and digital compositing for the film *Dinosaur* (2000). She also provided corporate training at Disney and Dreamworks animation. She received a doctoral degree from USC Rossier School of Education and continues to write and research.

Filming the Fantastic with Virtual Technology
Filmmaking on the Digital Backlot

Mark Sawicki and Juniko Moody

Routledge
Taylor & Francis Group

LONDON AND NEW YORK

First published 2020
by Routledge
2 Park Square, Milton Park, Abingdon, Oxon OX14 4RN

and by Routledge
52 Vanderbilt Avenue, New York, NY 10017

Routledge is an imprint of the Taylor & Francis Group, an informa business

British Library Cataloguing-in-Publication Data
A catalogue record for this book is available from the British Library

Library of Congress Cataloging-in-Publication Data
A catalog record has been requested for this book

ISBN: 978-0-367-35422-0 (hbk)
ISBN: 978-0-367-35421-3 (pbk)
ISBN: 978-0-429-33128-2 (ebk)

Typeset in Bembo
by Servis Filmsetting Ltd, Stockport, Cheshire

http://pactekviz.thinkific.com/courses/filming-the-fantastic-case-studies-1

For Tom, Torine, and Troy

For Tom who taught his younger brother to see beyond the stars.

For Juniko's sister Torine who left too soon.

A brother and sister who left indelible marks upon our lives.

For father Troy who encouraged pursuit of education for all.

Contents

Preface

Bill Taylor

As a long-time Visual Effects Supervisor and Cinematographer, I found these new developments of virtual stage tech to be fascinating. Since *Avatar* (2009), and subsequent high points like *The Jungle Book* (2016) and *The Lion King* (2019), the emphasis has been on capturing actors (and mocap performers) for post compositing, with the live preview functions employed primarily for real-time feedback for the artists and crew on stage.

Here the real-time composite *is the product*, so formidable difficulties in shooting, synchronization, and rendering must be overcome. I'm very keen to see the films that result!

The reader is fortunate in having Mark and Juniko to guide them through this complex story. I had the good fortune to work with Mark every day over several years and was impressed not only by his skills as a cameraman, but also by his abilities as a master explainer. His wry sense of humor is a welcome, leavening touch!

Bill Taylor ASC, VES

Acknowledgments

As with any broad-ranging endeavor, a book happens through the patience and generosity of so many people. First and foremost, Mark Sawicki would like to thank Irfan Merchant and his studio for introducing me to all the modern miracles I am able to share. I spent the better part of 2019 at his studio learning, documenting, and helping set up the marvelous gadgets. I learned from him an agile way of working and the value of Skype as we communicated across the globe with amazing engineers and technicians learning how to set up and operate all the toys. Years ago, Irfan was one of my students at University of California, Los Angeles (UCLA) extension and now the student has truly become the master. I also want to thank Andrew Angulo for his patient and to-the-point explanations of Unreal® and other digital wonders; Bill Taylor ASC, VES for his ongoing support and mentorship; David Sanger for his contributions to the field and support of my efforts; Matt Winston and his team from the Stan Winston School of Character Arts who supplied those great behind-the-scenes stills from *Terminator 2* (1991) and *Jurassic Park* (1993); Hannah Bianchini and her Microsoft team for capturing and rendering my hologram imagery; Dan India and the team at Qualisys; Jason Sapan of Holographic Studios and Lennart Wietzke of Raytrix for their contributions to the holography and light field section; inventor Eliot Mack from Lightcraft for his fabulous photogrammetry and Halide FX images; Aydemir Sahin and Ece Cevikel and their team from Zero Density for all their help and patiently teaching me the inner workings of the Reality™ system; Michael Geissler, Gary Attanasio, and the team at Mo-Sys for providing illustrations and explanation of the lens calibration process; Michael Foster and Olivia Chiesi for use of their considerable talent as artists and models for my illustrations. The authors would like to thank USC professors Alex McDowell and Mike Fink for their contributions and input; Producer Nancy Fulton who was witness to this journey and shares all things movie with her community meet-ups; Artist and educator Elizabeth Leister for her review and insights; our editor Emma Tyce and the good people at Routledge, Taylor and Francis Group who believed in the book. Thanks also to our manager Darla Marasco who cheered us on all the way.

Introduction

The dawn of the virtual studio

It will have been nearly a decade since the publication of the second edition of *Filming the Fantastic*. Since that time, I have seen amazing accomplishments in both the traditional and digital fields. In 2011 *Rise of the Planet of the Apes* was nominated for a Visual Effects Oscar for the spectacular work of creating realistic motion-capture (mocap) CGI apes performing alongside human actors. In 2014 Paul Franklin, Andrew Lockley, Ian Hunter, and Scott Fisher won the Best Achievement in Visual Effects Oscar for the film *Interstellar* where 99% of all the fantastic space sequences were done with traditional model photography. In 2016 the VFX Oscar went to Robert Legato, Adam Valdez, Andrew Jones, and Dan Lemmon for the amazing Disney film *Jungle Book* (2016) that combined a live-action Mowgli with ultra-realistic synthetic creatures and jungles. Within this short time span traditional VFX work has given way to highly iterative and interactive digital tools and at the same time the high pioneering price point for this technology has come down so that these visual effects are no longer the domain of the multimillion-dollar tentpole pictures that we have enjoyed so much. The independent filmmakers of today can now have access to new off-the-shelf systems to enhance or create amazing fantasy films.

Many of the traditional artists such as miniature model makers, optical camera persons, and the like have successfully transitioned to become Maya® and Unreal® artists or Adobe® After Effects® and Nuke™ compositors. Others such as Ian Hunter have gone on to become 360 cinema directors and producers forging ahead once again to break new ground in this exciting field.

I have had the fantastic opportunity to be on the ground floor of helping set up and document a state-of-the-art virtual studio, Mobile Motion MoCap. The owner, Irfan Merchant, has assembled a unique collection of off-the-shelf (not proprietary) software and hardware tools that make modern miracles of the screen possible and, in many cases, in real time! The purpose of this book is to not leave behind traditional disciplines but to understand those foundations better to build upon them and apply them to the new and flexible tools of today.

The key words here are "real time" as the virtual production process is rapidly becoming as streamlined as traditional filmmaking. The idea of shooting performers on a blank green stage and waiting weeks or months while the sets and synthetic characters are slowly developed or animated, and cameras tracked for compositing in post-production has given way to affordable off-the-shelf assets and live compositing with sets and characters manipulated with performance capture tools resulting in the production day's final output ready for the editing room.

So, buckle up and hang on tight as we rocket into the future of here and now to virtually *Film the Fantastic*.

Mark Sawicki
Atop Bear Mountain
Tehachapi, CA

To view additional material for this book, visit http://pactekviz.thinkific.com.

Chapter 1
The first magicians

Since the dawn of Cinema in the late 19th century, filmmakers have called upon visual effects artists to help realize dreams of fantasy, or to simply devise incredible cost-saving measures to enhance partial sets, or to create environments and creatures never seen. What follows is a list of some foundational techniques that have been used in the industry to create fantastic environments and characters.

Temporal displacement and double exposure

George Melies is considered by many to be the grandfather of visual effects from the silent era. His considerable contributions of technique included starting and stopping the camera to make objects seem to magically appear and disappear in the shot (having been placed or removed during the period that the camera was idle), fantasy imagery achieved through the painting of sets and flats and exposing the same film multiple times to create superimposition effects. These methods have been refined and are still in use even in the digital realm of today.

Matte painting and foreground miniature

One of the first techniques used to extend a set or introduce romantic atmosphere was the glass shot where an artist extended the scene by painting on a glass positioned at a point between the camera and the live-action set with the camera keeping both in focus. As the camera only has one eye and no depth perception the addition of a new roof, mountains, sky or other pictorial displays would be seamlessly blended with the live action if the camera did not move. If a pan was introduced the painting would "pull away" from the live action, revealing its small size and position. Early practitioners would avoid this problem by panning and/or tilting the camera on the nodal point of the lens where all the light rays converged within roughly the center of the lens. When camera movement was executed in this way both the glass painting and the background would remain "locked together" visually and not pull apart. This enabled camera movement but had the drawback of eliminating any perspective shift of foreground and background elements. It would be as if you panned and tilted while photographing a flat still image. Nonetheless the technique is very successful and is used today when executing panoramic photography. The main drawback of the glass shot was the time frame of execution. As most shots took place outdoors the final composite shot had to be taken at the same time of day that the painting was created in order to match the shadows drawn on the painting with the real shadows of the background. This issue was solved using foreground miniatures instead of flat art, which, being dimensional,

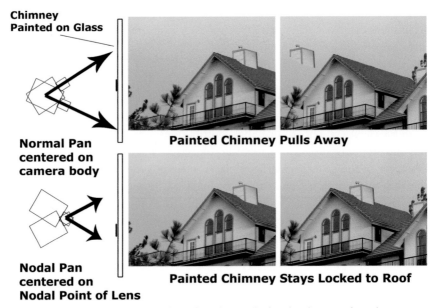

Figure 1.1 *The chimney painted on glass close to the lens breaks away from the alignment on the roof with a normal pan but stays locked in place when panned on the nodal point of the lens where all light rays converge.*

Figure 1.2 *An example of a foreground miniature composite. The join is where the miniature street meets the full-size curb in the background.*

would show the same shadows as those that appeared on the background live action as they were both illuminated by the same light source which would be the sun. While these methods were extremely effective, they were also time consuming in the production workflow.

Post production effects

The matte painter Norman Dawn developed a technique called the latent image matte painting that allowed for the time-consuming work of developing a painting to reside in the comfortable confines of a visual effect studio. The process entails setting a frame in front of the camera as was done with the glass shot technique but in this case the area to be occupied by the painting was masked off by black cards to create a matte. As film only records light and not darkness the area occupied by the opaque black matte has no effect on that area of the film as it remains unexposed to light. The live-action take could be executed very rapidly, and a long take of test footage was photographed as a working template to develop the painting. After photography, each take was isolated in separate cans along with the test footage and placed in a refrigerator to arrest any photo chemical change within the film. The rolls of film lay dormant awaiting a second exposure of the painting to fill the unexposed area of the film. A short clip of the photography was developed to check for exposure and focus and was also placed in a special matte camera that could double as a projector. The processed film was projected out onto an easel where the artist could see where the black matte area was located and begin blocking out the painting at leisure. The process of tracing from a projected photographed image is called rotoscoping (also referred to as roto). The bottom half of the painting was painted black so as not to contaminate the latent image of the live action that existed on the unprocessed takes. When the painting was ready the latent takes were loaded into the matte camera and a second exposure of the painting was photographed on top of the live-action takes. With careful painting and blending the painting would seamlessly combine with the live action and have the exact same first-generation quality (no film duplication needed) as a glass shot. This saved tremendous time in production and took a great deal of pressure off the artist.

Over the years this technique was used and refined by a long lineage of artists throughout the 20th century such as Percy Day, Peter Ellenshaw, Albert Whitlock, Harrison Ellenshaw, Syd Dutton, Mathew Yuricich, and Robert Stromberg, among others.

The drawback of this technique was the inability to move the camera as both photo elements were shot at different times and therefore difficult to synchronize any kind of camera movement. As a result, even the best matte painting

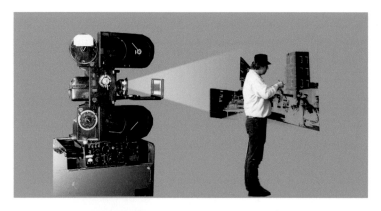

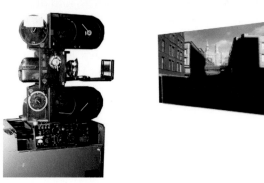

Figure 1.3 *The latent image matte painting process. The image above shows the camera being turned into a projector so that the rotoscoping process of tracing out the matte location and blocking in the painting begins. The bottom image shows the same instrument converted into a camera to photograph the finished matte painting with black on the bottom to protect the live-action exposure as the painting will be exposed on top of the latent image of the live action creating the composite shown in Figure 1.4.*

Figure 1.4 *The black area is the matte that prevents exposure in the upper part of the frame as the first step of the latent image matte painting technique. The completed matte painting below is incorporating a foreground miniature train. This was a test painting shot for the film* Entertaining Angels: The Dorothy Day Story *(1996) and was perhaps one of the last times the latent image technique was utilized. Painting by Robert Stromberg.*

stood out over the years due to the shots being static. As film duplication methods improved, large format latent image composites could have moves added in post but suffered slight degradation in the duplication process. The ideas of rotoscoping and the traditional art techniques of matching color, lighting and perspective continue today using Photoshop® and compositing software.

Rear projection and post movement techniques

The ability to copy film images without a severe reduction in quality gave rise to being able to move the camera again. Visual effects and stop-motion pioneer Willis O'Brien developed several methods involving rear projection techniques to create the RKO fantasy film *King Kong* in 1932. In the Stegosaurus sequence a small stop-motion model was animated while being sandwiched between a combination of miniature foregrounds and glass matte paintings to create a background performance that was then rear projected onto a large translucent screen behind the live-action actors. Both the projection and the live action were photographed together while allowing the camera to dolly in towards

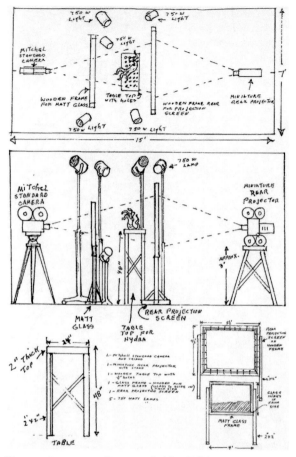

Figure 1.5 *Dynamation set-up. Courtesy Archive-Editions.com.*

the actors and the rear projected dinosaur to spectacular effect. Conversely, miniature sets, paintings and the King Kong model would have small portions of the settings (such as a cave opening) contain a rear projection screen where the live-action performance was projected a frame at a time into the animation set as the models were animated. The use of rear projection brought camera movement back as all elements (projection and live actors or stop-motion models) were locked together as they were photographed simultaneously. Lighting was challenging as light had to be prevented from striking the screen as it would wash out the background imagery. The big breakthrough of rear projection was the ability for the performers and the animator to see and react to the projected image to achieve wonderful interaction.

Willis O'Brien's protégé Ray Harryhausen built upon this method and created a technique called Dynamation where he used the latent image method of mattes to sandwich fantasy creatures into rear projected live-action settings.

Figure 1.6 *Rear projection afforded great interactive performance as the actor or animator could see the composite while they worked. The drawback of rear projection was the unavoidable quality difference between the subject (photographed for the first time) and the rear projected background which was being re-photographed. The background image always had an increase in contrast and grain when compared side by side with the subject.*

While this eliminated the need for building time-consuming miniature sets it had the drawback of requiring locked off shots like the latent image matte painting technique.

Re-photographing film using projection introduced an increase in grain and contrast along with a loss of definition. Some of these pitfalls were eliminated by creating a low-contrast projection element and using larger format films such as 65 mm or Vista Vision to reduce the grain and compensate for the contrast increase. The front projection system used throughout the 60s and 70s was a clever variation of rear projection that allowed for better definition and detail as the image was projected from the front instead of behind and through a screen. Front projection could also provide a much larger image due to the high light output afforded by the retroreflective process. It was most notably used for the Dawn of Man sequence in Stanley Kubrick's *2001: A Space Odyssey* (1968). Today LED video light panels are enabling rear projection concepts to make a comeback by providing interactive light for subjects as in the case of the film *Gravity* (2013) where the performers faces were lit by a large video wall displaying moving imagery to obtain elegant light interaction on the actors before their facial elements were inserted within CGI space suits. Projection technique maestros of the traditional era include Farciot Edouart ASC, John Eppolito (Introvision), Zoran Perisic (Zoptic system), Dennis Skotak (*Terminator 2: Judgment Day*, 1991), and Bill Hansard (*Moonraker*, 1979).

The optical printer

To improve film duplication, special optical printers were created that could copy film using macro photography rather than by the physical contact of film to film during exposure. These systems were makeshift devices in early cinema until Linwood Dunn ASC and Cecil Love were commissioned by the government to create a standardized printer for the Armed Forces Photography Units during World War II. After the war the equipment they produced was made available to studios and film laboratories. In 1944 Dunn and Love received an Academy Technical Achievement Award for "the design and construction of the Acme-Dunn Optical Printer." The team went on to receive the Gordon E. Sawyer Award for Highest Technical Achievement from the Academy in 1985. The optical printer they developed became the ultimate post process tool for motion pictures. The printer was the ubiquitous Adobe® After Effects® of the photo mechanical era.

Since the duplication method was a post process, exotic special-order films meant for duplication were used to raise the quality of the duplicate negative to be very close to the original. Using methods such as blue screen where the live-action element is extracted off a blue backing, one could create excellent composites by combining several pre-photographed elements. Since all the elements were duplicated at the same time in the same way they all blended together in color and detail. This was an improvement over rear projection where you always had a side-by-side comparison of original photography and a re-photographed film element off the screen.

Figure 1.7 *The optical printer developed and refined by Linwood Dunn and Cecil Love.*

The printer's lenses had precise positioning tools and gauges to measure the position of a lens to one-thousandth of an inch. Matte painting composites created with the latent image technique if done on a large format film process such as 65 mm or the 8 perforation Vista Vision format could be duplicated with high quality while animating the copy lens frame-by-frame to introduce pans and tilts thereby bringing back movement to matte paintings with the same effect as the panning on the nodal point method of the glass shot technique. Another benefit of the micro positioning of the lens was the ability to steady certain shots through cancelation. A bit of negative film was positioned in the eyepiece of the camera so that the operator could view the positive image being duplicated against the single negative image of the same shot. The taking lens would be positioned up/down and side-to-side until the positive and negative canceled each other out creating an even gray field. A single frame would be shot of the repositioned positive then move on to the next unsteady frame and the procedure was repeated. After this painstaking process the unsteady shot was rendered rock steady. The macro photography technique of film duplication allowed the ability to reposition, push in, color correct, vignette, blur, fade in and out, dissolve, matte titles and execute the scores of other effects that make up the visual grammar of the motion picture.

Blue screen and beyond

Methods for replacing a pure color screen behind performers with a background image has existed since the silent black-and-white era. One of the earliest methods was the Dunning Pomeroy process where a yellow dyed background image was placed in contact with the raw stock inside of a camera that was photographing a yellow lit performer in front of a blue screen. The yellow lit performer's image would project through the yellow dyed background image to expose the raw stock as if the background image was not there while the blue-screen area would increase the contrast of the yellow background image enabling it to be seen and printed "apparently" behind the figure.

When color came to the movies the blue-screen technique became used in films using optical printers as early as Alexander Korda's *Thief of Baghdad* (1940). While extremely useful and flexible, the technique constantly fought the appearance of the bright blue halo around the subject (displaying the original blue background) due to the photographic mattes inability to fit perfectly together.

In the late 50s the genius inventor Petro Vlahos solved the halo problem. In order to reproduce film in high quality, the original color negative was copied onto three black-and-white films. Once through a red filter that recorded all the red information in the image on one roll of black-and-white film, then once again on another black-and-white film through a green filter to obtain or

Figure 1.8 *The Dunning Pomeroy process.*

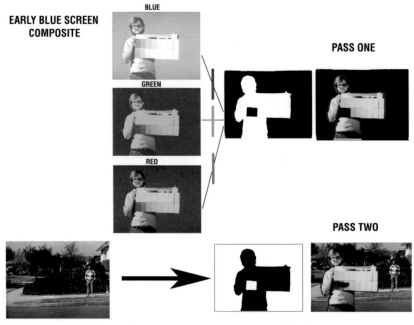

Figure 1.9 *The original blue-screen process where the use of the blue separation caused a blue fringe around the subject as seen in the final result.*

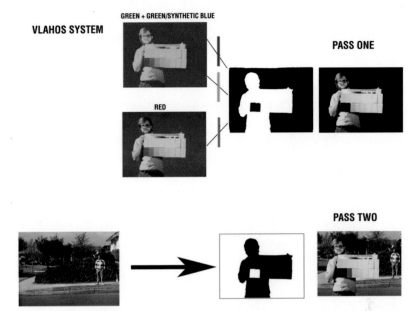

Figure 1.10 *The Vlahos system made use of the blue record for the mask creation only but filled in the color of the subject using only the red and green records where the green separation was exposed twice—once with a green filter and then a blue filter—to totally eliminate the halo effect.*

"record" the green information, and then once more for the blue information so to obtain three rolls of black-and-white film that contained the separated records of the color. These black-and-white films were then re-photographed onto color film through their corresponding red, green, and blue filters in three separate exposures to obtain high quality reproductions of the original film. The black-and-white film was much finer in detail than color film and allowed for the technical trick of isolating the blue to obtain a matte. Vlahos deduced that the blue record that had the problematic clear area in the blue-screen part of the image was only needed to create the matte, and the black-and-white green record could be used for both the blue and green information.

Vlahos' color difference process eliminated the issue of the blue halo and allowed the blue-screen technique to become one of the leading compositing tools of the movies. This remarkable inventor also developed the Sodium vapor process (used in Disney's *Mary Poppins* (1964)) that allowed for the use of any color (even blue) to be rendered in the foreground image of the composite as the process derived its elements from a special technicolor camera (that could record two film strips simultaneously) that used a prism that separated the image of the performer from the narrow wavelength sodium screen (blocked by a special filter) to create a full color performer against a black screen on one roll of film while the other image reflected and filtered by the prism created the matte on the other film roll that only exposed the narrow wavelength sodium light leaving a perfect silhouette of the actor. The final composite was executed on the optical printer.

Incredibly, Vlahos went on to perfect his color difference process for video when he founded the Ultimatte Corporation. Ultimatte became the leading color compositing tool in the industry and brought about the ability to use green as well as blue in the electronic medium to generate flawless composites. In the 90s, Ultimatte went on to create software for high fidelity digital film applications and invented the clean plate comparison system to enable excellent composites even under marginal lighting conditions. This comparison method is now used in the Zero Density Reality™ system we will examine in later chapters. Petro Vlahos and Ultimatte were a pioneering force behind many of the virtual backlot techniques we will examine later.

The list of brilliant camera operators and directors of photography to refine optical work and blue screen include Clarence Slifer ASC, L.B. Abbott ASC, Howard A. Anderson ASC, Frank Van der Veer ASC, Bill Taylor ASC, Art Cruickshank ASC, and Richard Edlund ASC, among others.

Figure 1.11 *The use of blue screen and the optical printer allowed for high-quality composites without the direct comparison of first- and second-generated elements that came with projection methods. Due to the fidelity of digital we can now use green screens as well.*
    Red can also be used but is seldom utilized for human subjects as there is so much red color in skin tones. The woman was shot in front of a blue screen for this television commercial. Her reflection was created by flipping her image upside down and double exposing her image atop the floor yielding the transparent effect, while her image above is solid as the matte generated from the blue screen held back the image of the background.

The animation stand

Animation stands have long been the workhorse of cartoon and visual effects production as the camera and art platform was designed to be positioned with repeatable precision. An example of how the repeatability of the device was used for visual effects can be seen in the work of Zoran Perisic in the film *2001: A Space Odyssey* (1968). The opening space sequence showing satellites orbiting the Earth was executed in the following manner. The camera was loaded with color film and a hole punch was made in the film to indicate the "zero" frame and the counter was adjusted accordingly to zero. A still photograph of a satellite model was laid atop a black background on the animation stand and a synthetic move was made by animating the camera pushing in on the art while moving the photograph along the X/Y axis using cranks. Each positioner would have a numerical read out of the camera and artwork position. These numbers would be written down on a shot sheet so they could be replicated later. After photography the color film was removed and placed in a refrigerator and held latent much like the Norman Dawn process. At this point the still photograph was painted white against the black background and the camera was loaded with high contrast black-and-white stock that again had a zero hole punch made in the film. Now the exact same animation move was repeated a frame at a time, number-by-number, as indicated on the shot sheet. After photography the black-and-white film was processed yielding a black silhouette of the satellite on clear film creating a "traveling matte," meaning

Figure 1.12 *Today the Perisic method can be accomplished effortlessly in After Effects® by making an element in Photoshop® that has one layer that includes the picture of the spacecraft and its alpha channel (matte). It is like having art pasted to a sheet of glass above the Earth layer much like the Disney Multiplane camera made in the 30s with the exception that you have no limitation of size and positioning as you are not restricted by physical space. The spacecraft can be reduced to the size of a pin point if needed.*

a matte that changed its shape or position frame-by-frame. This matte was loaded together with the latent color film in a method called bi packing where the processed black-and-white matte film was placed in contact and in front of the partially exposed color film and loaded together in the camera. The matte prevented re-exposure of the satellite image and allowed for the photography of the Earth behind the satellite. During photography of the Earth the camera would either be static or have an entirely different counter move for the Earth, introducing an apparent dimensional move. Once again both elements were the same generation and quality, yielding an exceptional composite. The idea of precise coordinates for both camera and artwork along with the frame-by-frame process of animation was the direct precursor to the introduction of the computer and motion-control techniques.

Motion control and the introduction of computers

Motion control is a method of using a computer to position cameras and artwork precisely by sending commands to stepper motors that were engineered to repeat positions with extreme accuracy. While the first known use of motion control was *Sampson and Delilah* (1949) using sound equipment to record motor signals, the big breakthrough came with the introduction of

Figure 1.13 *A motion-controlled camera rig with the lens positioned on the nodal point. Designed by Bill Taylor ASC.*

computers for the films *Star Wars* and *Close Encounters of the Third Kind* both made in 1977. The Dykstraflex named after VFX supervisor John Dykstra and used for Star Wars was in many ways the painstaking Perisic technique accelerated a thousand-fold. The camera could not only move but repeat the move exactly or repeat the move with scaled dimensions such as pushing in on a live-action actor against blue screen and using the optical printer to combine that shot with an identical move made on a miniature with a scaled-down move, meaning that if the live-action camera moved 40 feet on the live actor the move on a ¼ scale model had the camera move only 10 feet. The integration was flawless and dynamic as these computer-controlled cameras could seamlessly combine moving camera elements photographed in the real world. This same technology was also added to animation stands and optical printers to enable flawless repeatability for multi-element composite shots. The motion-control pioneers include John Dykstra, Doug Trumbull, Bob Abel, Al Miller, Paul Johnson, Jerry Jeffress, and Ray Feeney, among others.

Introduction of digital compositing

In the early 90s Eastman Kodak introduced the Cineon system that was one of the first commercially available high-end digital compositing tools. The system was composed of a scanner that translated the image on motion picture film into digital information. The engineers determined that in order to reproduce the resolution of 35 mm motion picture film, one needed to derive a file from the scanner that was 4096 × 3112 pixels encoding each pixel with a 10-bit log color space that allowed for 1024 levels of color per channel. By comparison a typical standard digital video of the time was 720 × 486 pixels with an 8-bit linear color space that only had available 256 levels of color per channel. When the raw Cineon file was viewed on a monitor it appeared to have very low contrast which caused no end of consternation to traditional film workers who struggled to grasp the new digital technology. It all became clear when one realized that the low contrast Cineon file had the same contrast as a film negative with the exception that it was a positive image. After processing through the Cineon software pipeline, one could make corrections while viewing the data in "print" form where the contrast was adjusted to create a customary normal contrast view. The final output, much like the optical printer film pipeline, became a digital negative intermediate file that could be output onto film using the Kodak laser scanner where red, green, and blue lasers wrote the image onto the final film negative pixel-by-pixel. The low contrast appearance of raw files still occurs today with modern digital negative files from the RED camera (.r3d), Arri Alexa camera (.arri), Sony camera (.sr2) and others. At first glance the images look incorrectly exposed until one realizes they are raw data. There was never a confusion when we worked with an orange tinted negative from the traditional film days.

Cineon software and output

The Cineon system introduced a node-based process where image manipulation tools were compartmentalized into discreet units. Many of the tools were based on the Optical camera tool set. Instead of physically "flopping" the film, a node was created that rearranged the pixel order to accomplish the same thing, but only to perform that one operation. Another node might be a tool that adjusted focus and so on. The structure was brilliant as it allowed for fine tuning the pipeline by adding or eliminating nodes across a wide web of processes. Though powerful, it did not become popular at the outset as Cineon competed with systems that used layer methodology such as After Effects®. The Flame system was a strong competitor for Cineon at the time, especially when it developed into the Inferno system that could handle film resolution composites. Today the node-based architecture has taken hold as the primary methodology for current systems such as Nuke™ and the Reality™ system that we will examine later in the book.

Motion control gives way to motion tracking

While motion control was a huge boon to visual effects by combining moving camera elements together, it began to lose favor as a method for recording camera motion and became replaced by image analysis systems. Motion-control techniques can be expensive and time consuming to have on a production and they potentially create another point of failure in the pipeline should the data become corrupted. As a result, artists would turn to tracking marks on blue screens and tennis balls thrown on the ground to serve as camera motion reference points. These tracking markers would be used in software to backward analyze what the live camera positions were and then introduce that data to virtual cameras inside software to virtually "photograph" the computer graphic characters or backgrounds in the same manner so that they could be composited easily. While the virtual camera can move in the same way as the live camera, it was soon discovered that the perfect virtual lens would need to be custom created to have the same distortions as the lens used in the original

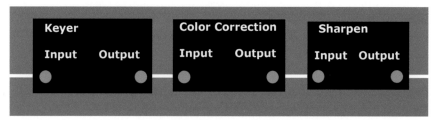

Figure 1.14 *In a node system each box had a specific function. Clicking on the box would open up a number of controls to fine tune the function such as color correction, which would open up to reveal sliders to control the red, green, and blue levels of an image.*

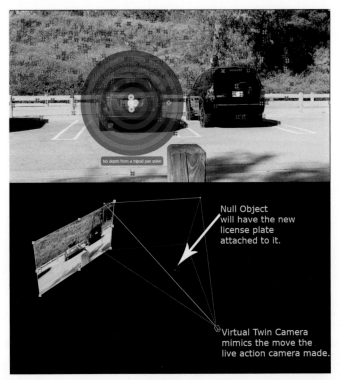

No depth from a tripod pan solve

Null Object will have the new license plate attached to it.

Virtual Twin Camera mimics the move the live action camera made.

Figure 1.15 *Motion tracking relies on the location of contrast points and dimensional changes from frame to frame to derive the lens used and how the live-action camera moved in order to generate a matching synthetic camera. In this case, the bullseye centers around track points that have centered around the license plate in order to create a "Null object".*

The bottom view shows the virtual camera created from the tracking data that has the same lens and movement as the real camera. The null object is placed at the same distance from the virtual camera as the real license plate was from the real camera. A false license plate is attached to the null which then will cover the real plate and continue to cover it throughout the camera move. Adobe® product screenshot reprinted with permission from Adobe®.

photography. The ability to post track camera movement and composite using virtual elements has led to a rapid live-action workflow but a very long post pipeline involving an incredible number of artists to generate the visuals.

Character creation

As was pointed out earlier, the matte painting was the go-to tool for set extension and more importantly to create amazing environments that could not be easily realized in a practical sense. One could paint anything and create subtle movements within the art to make it come alive. Fantastic characters that had to interact with performers brought about the art of fantasy makeup

Figure 1.16 *The great Lon Chaney Sr. portraying the amputee Blizzard in* The Penalty *(1920, Universal Studios). He achieved this amazing illusion by performing with his lower legs bent back and bound to his thighs.*

Figure 1.17 *Stan Winston and Stephen Spielberg alongside a crew member and a full-size dinosaur creation for the film* Jurassic Park. Jurassic Park *behind-the-scenes images courtesy of Stan Winston School of Character Arts.*

and creature creation. Lon Chaney Sr. is considered the grandfather of effects makeup with his incredible portfolio of work such as *The Phantom of the Opera* (1925) and *The Hunchback of Notre Dame* (1923), among others. Makeup effects were refined throughout the years by artists such as Jack Pierce (*Frankenstein,*

1931), John Chambers (*Planet of the Apes*, 1968), Dick Smith (*The Exorcist*, 1973), Rick Baker (*Men in Black*, 1997), and Stan Winston (*The Terminator*, 1984, and *Jurassic Park*, 1993).

The creation of giant-sized creatures was extremely challenging. The Dragon in Fritz Lang's *Die Nibelungen: Siegfried* (1924) for example was 60 feet long and required 17 technicians to operate it. Over the years technological improvements improved the look of giant-sized animatronics culminating in the amazing full-size dinosaur effects done by Stan Winston on *Jurassic Park*.

The most successful attempts at creating giant-sized creatures before computer graphics were through the use of stop-motion animation and compositing puppets within live action through the use of rear projection technique as done by Willis O'Brien (*King Kong*, 1933), Ray Harryhausen (*Jason and the Argonauts*, 1963), Jim Danforth (*When Dinosaurs Ruled the Earth*, 1970), and Phil Tippet (*Dragonslayer*, 1981).

The forced perspective technique was particularly effective for combining different sized human actors together by merely placing one performer further back from the camera than the other and through clever art direction making them seem to be on the same plane with one being much larger than the other.

Figure 1.18 *One of my favorite effects from the traditional era for creating characters of unusual size is forced perspective. The above composites demonstrate how big our dog Oscar thinks he is while the set-up below reveals the truth. Oscar is placed closer to the camera and elevated while standing on the same material that is under my feet. With proper lighting and art-directed blending of the platform and flooring we create the illusion that we buy a lot of dog food.*

Figure 1.19 *The amazing T-Rex creation and the crew of the Stan Winston studio.* Jurassic Park *behind-the-scenes images courtesy of Stan Winston School of Character Arts.*

Wonderful examples of this can be found in Peter Ellenshaw's stunning work in the Disney film *Darby O'Gill and the Little People* (1959) where the illusion of leprechauns performing alongside a full-size human were shot all at one time without the need of any post work. A more recent example can also be found in the amazing Lord of the Rings trilogy (2001–2003) where the technique was used to combine the different-sized wizards, elves, gnomes, and hobbits.

Even with the advent of digital compositing, all visual effects involved the direct shooting and compositing of real-world elements together, be they miniatures, models, matte paintings, makeup or puppets. In films such as *Terminator 2* (1991) and *Jurassic Park* (1993) we were witness to the amazing introduction of virtual character creations made up of algorithms, polygons and coordinates within computer graphics. This change was as profound as the transition from silent to sound movies for the VFX industry. The next chapter will trace the history and concepts behind the computer graphic miracles we enjoy today and enable us a better understanding of the processes we will be using in our later chapters as we explore the virtual backlot movie studio.

Chapter 2
A brief history of computer graphics

The complexity of the topic

For the purposes of this chapter and due to space constraints, most developments discussed are in prominent and/or multiple sources found in the United States. If space permitted, there would be many more US and global contributors covered.

This chapter uses a simplified framework designed to briefly list highlights and the environment leading up to our modern-day photo-realistic and hyper-realistic computer-generated imagery (CGI). It is a long and convoluted path in which computer graphics (CG) would eventually become undetectable from reality.

The history of CGI is primarily driven by the development of the computer (in general) and the personal computer (specifically) and involves an accumulation of factors consisting of the concerted effort of innovative individuals, military and corporate finance, technological invention, and even some counter-culture psychedelic imaginings and early hacking. Visualization became a priority early in computer development when numbers and text were acknowledged as insufficient methods to fulfill other purposes that needed to be included in a general tool such as was desired of the computer. While these early purposes may have been less entertainment related, there were entertainment efforts throughout both the development of the computer and the personal computer. Eventually, entertainment became the most well-recognized and the highest-profile CGI use.

Visualization needs as found in defense, manufacturing, education, and science required graphic depiction of abstract concepts, processes, procedures, and design. To understand how CGI use evolved in entertainment, and especially movies, it is important to follow the technological development of computer visualization, which includes not only technology but a collusion of people and ideas.

Simply put, the evolution of computer-generated imagery that allowed increasingly realistic capture of our physical world progressed through the following stages:

1. Simple geometric wireframes of objects.
2. Depiction of visible and hidden surfaces of objects.
3. Surface shading (material), texture, and transparency of objects.
4. Simulation of light properties such as ray tracing, radiosity, reflection, refraction, and dispersion.
5. Simulation of physics forces, physical properties, and natural elements such as gravity, acceleration, friction, resistance, tension, spring, collision, wind, turbulence, fire, water, plants, volumetric properties, and particle control.
6. Simulation of human and animal motion such as walking, running, climbing, falling, jumping, flocking, flying, and swimming. This includes simulation of motion utilizing rendering and post-process procedures such as motion blur and other techniques necessary to display natural and perceived motion.
7. The use of scientific properties of human and animal anatomy such as hair, skin, feathers, fur, and liquids that allowed for photo-realistic creation of humans and animals in interaction and reaction to the physics forces and natural elements listed above.
8. Digital image processing advancements such as compositing (as in blue/green screen and image layering), rendering (especially faster calculations, specialty procedures for surface, light, materials, and motion), and display improvements for higher resolution results.
9. Real-time high-fidelity calculation and display to complete all of the above processes (the Holy Grail of 3D or three-dimensional graphics: real-time procedural display).

Figure 2.1 shows the complexity of environmental contributing factors leading up to today's hyper-real CGI. While this timeline is an approximation of

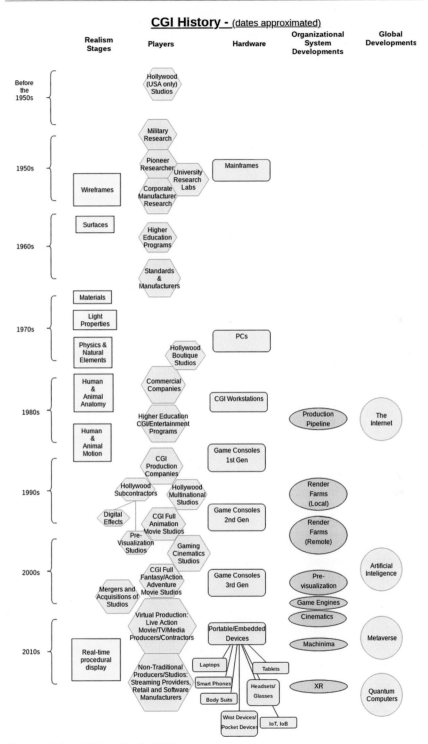

Figure 2.1 *CGI timeline highlights.*

the decades leading up to and involving the evolution of modern CGI use, contributing factors include: the nine realism stages listed above; the players involved in computer and computer graphics technology development and usage; hardware developments; computer networking system milestones; and widespread global achievements and influences.

Before the 1950s – calculators and electromechanics

The period of time before the 1950s represents early pioneering into the concept of a computer and reflects human understanding in the use of devices such as a calculator and typewriter. Early calculators in the form of the abacus for counting or slide rule for higher math functions like multiplication, division, and trigonometry were among many early math tools. In the 1800s the difference engine and the analytical engine were invented by Charles Babbage in England. The difference engine calculated 20- to 30-digit mathematical tables. The analytical engine had the four basic components used by computers to this day: a mill (or central processing unit/CPU), storage, a reader (data input), and a printer (data output). Babbage's assistant, Augusta Ada Lovelace, is credited with the fifth component of modern computers, which is programming. The programming language ADA is named after her. Also invented in the 1880s was the typewriter.

The concept of machine intelligence in which a computer could learn from experience and solve problems using logic was introduced by Alan Turing of England in the form of the universal Turing machine in 1936. This was actually an abstract model and not a physical machine, however Turing is credited with one of the first public lectures describing computer intelligence as a forerunner to artificial intelligence.

Meanwhile, during the turn of the 20th century there were multiple electronic discoveries and inventions helping to advance calculators and typewriters away from purely mechanical contraptions to electromechanical devices (any mechanics powered by electricity). Electromechanical devices pre-date modern electronics that have few moving parts. Miniaturization (e.g. transistors) of electromechanical components allowed for the shift from analog to digital involving microelectronics; the foundation of all our present-day communication and design equipment.

The 1950s – electronics

After the pioneers of electricity and computers, from the 1950s to today, came multiple innovators, adaptors, and followers. This decade marks the birth of the Internet; early computer software; the merging of technology, art and design; and the first use of electronic graphics in a movie title sequence and video game. This period begins with US federal government and military interest in new technologies.

In 1957 Sputnik launched to become Earth's first satellite. Not to be out-done, the United States, under President Dwight D. Eisenhower, formed the Advanced Research Projects Agency (ARPA) in 1958 for the purpose of expanding research into technology and science. NASA was established in 1958 and requisitioned most of ARPA's funds but later all civilian space programs would be transferred to NASA freeing ARPA to concentrate on more risky and innovative projects in areas such as computer processing and behavioral science. Out of this research would come the kernel of an idea leading to the Internet.

Mainframe computers were being developed by military divisions in coordi-nation with corporations and/or universities. The Navy's Airplane Stability and Control Analyzer (ASCA) in conjunction with MIT began development on the Whirlwind computer in the 1940s and was demonstrated in 1951 for a flight simulation environment. The US Air Force used Whirlwind in its Semi-Automatic Ground Environment (SAGE) air defense system in 1958. Whirlwind and SAGE used the cathode ray tube (CRT) display as an interac-tive device with the introduction of a light pen.

There were many mainframe manufacturers including IBM, Univac, Honeywell, RCA, and General Electric. Mainframes were extremely large computers (e.g. room-sized) and extremely expensive so had only commercial applications and were not available to the general public. (It would take the invention of the personal computer to make computers small and relatively inexpensive enough for public availability.) With the involvement of com-mercial manufacturers, the computer and the computer graphic industries had officially begun.

Grace Hopper was a distinguished programmer working with the ENIAC mainframe who published a paper in 1952 providing the foundation for com-puter language and programming. This was the beginning of the concept of software reusability and applications. Her efforts assisted in the widespread use of computers by people who are not programmers. Admiral Hopper received many awards including the Computer Science Man-of-the-Year Award (1969) and was made a Distinguished Fellow of the British Computer Society (1973).

Analog displays using CRTs or oscilloscopes were viable displays, they resulted in experimental graphics, and were even used for one of the first video games called *Tennis for Two* presented in 1958 and created by William Higinbotham at Brookhaven National Laboratory in Upton, New York. *Tennis for Two* is widely accepted by some as the first interactive electronic game predating *Pong* and William Higinbotham has been dubbed the Grandfather of Video Games by David H. Ahl, the editor of *Creative Computing* magazine.

John Whitney Sr. was a filmmaker who blended artistry and analog computers with CRT displays to create mostly abstract imagery. Using a film camera, Whitney would photograph the moving images off the video screen resulting in the ability to use traditional film methods to create his animations. With graphic artist Saul Bass, Whitney created the first vector animation movie title sequence for Alfred Hitchcock's *Vertigo* in 1958. Vector animation is the use of lines and curves to create moving patterns. This began the commercial use of electronically created motion graphics for movies and broadcast.

In 1959 General Motors (GM) demonstrated the use of a digital design system (DAC-1) to store and manipulate auto design drawings. GM partnered with IBM to create specified software so that the IBM 7090 mainframe computer would have a graphics console, light pen, and be able to move, rotate, and manipulate drawings. This is the most noted use of commercial computer-aided design (CAD) in manufacturing at this time in the US.

By 1959 it was becoming clear that the computer could be a general-purpose tool. At this time, the New York Institute of Technology (NYIT) introduced mainframes as a teaching tool for physics, mathematics, and electronic instruction. NYIT sought to balance science and engineering education with liberal arts towards a career-oriented instructional strategy targeting veterans retraining for civilian life. This philosophy is maintained to date and is coupled with the beginning of the computer classroom and computer-assisted learning (CAL).

The 1960s – art and science

Continuing with the collaboration between military, corporate, and university entities, this decade sees the emergence of major computer and computer graphics developments due to legitimization of these industries. There are many "firsts" during this period. Prominent individuals arise who will influence computer development and CGI for decades to come. Millions of military and corporate dollars are devoted to establishing dominance over an arena that promises not only national but global advantages. Universities create computer graphic departments and there is an awareness that standards and practices need to be established. Wireframe animation ignites everyone's imagination and the most integral elements of the personal computer are demonstrated to influence Apple and Microsoft inventors. The decade ends with the first Internet transmission.

The first wireframe model of a human body was supervised by art director William Fetter for the Boeing Company in Seattle, Washington, in 1964. It became known as Boeing Man and was used in airplane cockpit design. Fetter also coined the term "computer graphics" with his supervisor Verne Hudson. The figures were drawn with a plotter (mechanical drawing arm) controlled by a computer. The series of drawings were novel in the use of 3D views of a human body in a series of poses. Some series of still images were filmed to create animation. Note that the use of the term 3D here refers to the depiction of form in dimensional and perspective views. Although the term 3D is also used when referring to stereoscopic view (usually requiring special eyeglasses and/or displays) that simulates our depth perception, in computer graphics this term usually refers to geometric dimensionality consisting of object height, width, and depth. Fetter continued using art and technology to participate in the International Art and Technology movement of the 1960s and helped found the Seattle chapter of Experiments in Art and Technology (E.A.T.) at the Henry Art Gallery in 1968.

In 1963 the first software for interactive CAD purposes, Sketchpad, was released. This application originated as computer graphics pioneer Ivan Sutherland's PhD thesis and was developed at MIT. Sketchpad breakthroughs included the first graphical user interface (GUI); the ability to duplicate "master" objects and drawings; instant updates to the duplicates when the master was modified; geometric constraints for accurate drafting of lines and angles; and a light pen used to draw directly on the monitor screen. Sketchpad was a precursor to the many CAD drafting programs available today and drafting programs led to the development of current 3D animation programs such as Maya®.

Sutherland and his associates comprise the who's who list of major participants in the early computer and computer graphics industries. In addition to MIT, he attended the Carnegie Institute of Technology and California Institute of Technology (Caltech). He was Associate Professor of Electrical Engineering at Harvard University; served for the Department of Defense ARPA's Information Processing Techniques Office (IPTO); co-founded the computer graphics firm, Evans and Sutherland with David Evans (founder of the Computer Science Department at the University of Utah); Professor of Computer Science at Caltech; Fellow and Vice President at Sun Microsystems; and a visiting scholar in the Computer Science Division at University of California, Berkeley.

Through the University of Utah's (Utah) newly formed Computer Science Department in 1968 chaired by David Evans, military involvement and funding led to the growth of ARPANET (early Internet) and an eclectic and cutting-edge group of computer scientists and engineers ready to build the technology of tomorrow. Illustrious alumni of the University of Utah include, but are not limited to, Edwin Catmull (Pixar, Walt Disney Animation), Jim Blinn (NASA's JPL, Microsoft, Caltech, Blinn shading, Carl Sagan's Cosmos), Jim Clark (Silicon Graphics, Netscape), Michael Cohen (Microsoft, Facebook), Alan Ashton (WordPerfect), Henri Gouraud (Gouraud shading), Bui Tuong Phong (Phong shading), John Warnock (Adobe®, PostScript language, PDF, hidden surface determination, Xerox PARC), and Martin Newell (Utah Teapot).

Sutherland and Bob Sproull (Oracle, Xerox PARC, *Principles of Interactive Computer Graphics* "the first bible of CGI" co-authored with William Newman, Sun Microsystems) invented the first virtual reality (VR) head-mounted display (HMD) system called the Sword of Damocles in 1968. Also, in 1968, Sutherland with David Evans formed Evans & Sutherland (E&S), a computer firm specializing in products for the military and industrial training and simulation. E&S employees were either alumni of Utah or associates of Evans and Sutherland such as Jim Clark (Utah, Silicon Graphics), Ed Catmull (Utah, Pixar), John Warnock (Utah, Adobe®), and Scott P. Hunter (Oracle).

Another school, Ohio State University (OSU), was experimenting with computer graphics and digital fine art. Charles Csuri was a pioneer computer artist and an art department faculty member of OSU. At OSU he would eventually become a Professor of Art Education in 1978 and a Professor of Computer Information Science in 1986. OSU focused on animation languages, modeling environments, user interfaces, and human and creature motion. OSU's CG research lab was funded by the National Science Foundation and government and private entities. The Computer Graphics Research Group (CGRG) was proposed by Csuri in 1971 and the collective art, math, and computer science students and faculty would produce several animated videos from the 1960s to the 1990s. (Later, Csuri would form the commercial production company, Cranston/Csuri, in the 1980s utilizing the students of CGRG.)

The Mother of All Demos was a demonstration given by Douglas Engelbart in 1968 at the Association for Computing Machinery/Institute of Electrical and Electronics Engineers (ACM/IEEE) conference, which showed what a complete computer system should look like and how it should perform. It captured all the essential functions of the personal computer including a mouse, windows, hypertext, graphics, navigation, command input, file linking, file revision control, word processing, and collaborative editing. It was called the NLS (oN-Line System), developed by the Augmentation Research Center (ARC) at Stanford University under Douglas Engelbart with funding primarily from ARPA. Engelbart's vision of the computer was a communication tool and for information retrieval. Already, the computer is starting to reach beyond being merely a calculator and typewriter to a device that could augment human thinking. Many of Engelbart's team would leave ARC to join the Xerox Palo Alto Research Center (PARC) to work on the Xerox Alto (arguably the first personal computer released in 1973 and Steve Jobs would study the Alto around the time of founding Apple in 1976). Attending the presentation was Andries van Dam who would later become a prominent CGI teacher in the 1970s and co-author the textbook, *Computer Graphics: Principles and Practice*, "the second bible of CGI," in 1982.

Some of the most important first results involving the photo-realistic stages of CGI development were being researched at the Utah Computer Science Department and would be ongoing throughout the following decades. Limitations related to image rendering became known as problems with visibility and led to improvements in wireframe presentations, hidden line, surface displays, and hidden surfaces. While wireframe models and animation were useful for scientific purposes, seeing the backside of objects was visually messy. Lines may also be hidden by the object itself or other objects in front.

Hidden line removal theories and algorithms that would help display only the lines and/or surfaces visible to the viewer were essential to realistic modeling and to save on computational time and memory. Hidden line removal was targeted as one of Ivan Sutherland's "Computer graphics: ten unsolved problems" (*Datamation*, 1966, 12(5):22–27). While researched at Utah, the first known solution was proposed by L.G. Roberts ("Machine perception of three-dimensional solids") in a PhD thesis at MIT in 1963. Over the years hidden line removal would continue to be refined.

Pierre Étienne Bézier, a French engineer worked for the auto manufacturer Renault in the 1960s and was one of the founders using curves in automobile design for CAD systems. He subsequently patented and popularized the Bézier curves and surfaces used in most modeling systems today. The resultant calculation of surfaces using parametric curves and splines led to the need for hidden surface removal (HSR). Most techniques dealing in hidden lines and surfaces involve sorting. Graphic elements must be sorted to determine which are visible, which are not visible, which should be calculated and displayed. A scan-line HSR algorithm was developed by Sutherland's associates Wylie, Romney, Evans, and Erdahl in 1967. The divide and conquer method was used to sort polygons that would be visible in the display. John Warnock (Utah) invented a hidden surface algorithm explained in his PhD thesis based on area subdivision.

The first ray casting algorithm was written by Arthur Appel in 1968. Based on drawing rays from the eye at one per pixel. It finds the closest object blocking the path of that ray and displays that surface while blocking all others behind it.

All this sorting and calculating to determine what should be displayed could not be executed without a memory intensive frame buffer which was invented in 1969 for Bell Labs. The frame buffer used memory to store image information before displaying on a monitor. This allowed for rapid data reading and refreshing to convert to images on a video screen. As we will see in the upcoming decade, the conversion of geometric data, mathematical selectivity, and video image conversion is refined even further to simulate reality.

The 1970s: rapid advancements in visualization and computer mass production

During this decade there are dynamic cultural influences as the rise of the personal computer and the Internet decentralized military and corporate tech-nological authority while paving the way for cyberculture. (Cyberculture is the social impact that computer network communication has on groups of users who form online communities. The Internet has been a major contributor in the formation of social media and communication allowing people with shared interests, biases, and/or style of conversation to gather and form cultural virtual spaces.) The first Internet Service Provider (ISP) in the form of TELENET (a commercial version of ARPANET) was released to the public in 1974. In 2006, author Fred Turner looked back at this pivotal time in his book *From Counterculture to Cyberculture: Stewart Brand, the Whole Earth Network, and the Rise of Digital Utopianism* (University of Chicago Press). Turner connects coun-terculture to cyberculture by suggesting that Stewart Brand (editor of the *Whole Earth Catalog* and founder of one of the first Internet forums, the WELL) had a major impact on the cyberculture movement. Counterculture perspectives were instrumental in merging art and design with computer technology and also in democratizing computer technology which spearheaded the invention of the personal computer and computer mass production. Steve Jobs promoted Apple as a counterculture computer company and the rift between military/corporate technological domination and grass roots technology for the masses becomes as wide as the distance between the east and west coasts of the USA. ARPA changes its name to DARPA (Defense Advanced Research Projects Agency) and Xerox PARC becomes PARC (Palo Alto Research Center). California takes prominence over corporate-led computer/software innova-tions due to free-thinking programming upstarts like Bill Gates, Paul Allen, Steve Jobs, Steve Wozniak, and the Homebrew Computer Club – hence Silicon Valley is born.

The first personal computers (PCs) are released and major advances in surface descriptions such as shading, materials, and lighting make photo-realism achievable. The first commercial frame buffer is offered through Evans & Sutherland and raster graphics become more widely used. (Evans & Sutherland also had a line of image generators that created displayed graphics without a framebuffer by generating images one line at a time or using scanline rendering. This was for real-time rendering.) The process of getting numerical and geometric data from the frame buffer to a monitor display is called rendering (visible surface determination) and rendering to not only sort which elements can be seen by a viewer but including simulation of realistic surfaces, materials, and lighting is a process that starts to develop rapidly.

The first SIGGRAPH (Special Interest Group on Computer Graphics and Interactive Techniques, subdivision of the Association for Computing Machinery) conference was assembled in 1974 to address standards and developments in computer graphics and an offshoot organization, the National Computer Graphics Association (NCGA), was founded in 1979 by Joel Orr and Peter Preuss. Movies like *Westworld* (1973), *Futureworld* (1976), *Star Wars* (1977), *Superman: The Movie* (1978), *Alien* (1979), *Star Trek* (1979), and *The Black Hole* (1979) used raster graphics as titles and/or special effects. Arcade games like *Pong* and *Pac-Man*, became extremely popular.

CGI surfaces were the main focus in the 1970s and The "Utah Teapot" by Martin Newell in 1975 became the ubiquitous test model for surface renders. A teapot was chosen because of its complex geometry consisting of symmetric and nonsymmetric forms, open areas, fat and skinny shapes, orientable (having a definitive front and a back), and self-shadowing properties. It became the benchmark for testing shaders, maps, and light effects. Bezier patches were used to model the teapot so that it had a smooth surface. Polygon surfaces look faceted but surfaces calculated with curves became the desired method of modeling. This required a different type of shading other than flat shading used for faceted surfaces.

Gouraud shading in 1971, named after Henri Gouraud (Utah), produces continuous shading of surfaces accomplished by using polygon vertices and interpolating the intensity values across the polygon and across adjacent polygons. This was good for dull or diffuse surfaces. Later, Bui-Tuong Phong (Utah) developed Phong shading that produced better highlights appropriate for shiny surfaces but they took longer to calculate. Different shaders simulate different surfaces (e.g. dull like cloth, glossy, and plastic) and specular highlights (e.g. dots and irregular shapes). These included the Blinn–Phong and later Lambert and Oren-Nayer.

Wolfgang Straßer (Germany) and Edwin Catmull (Utah, Disney, Pixar) developed z-buffering (depth buffering), which is another approach to solving the visibility problem (i.e. which pixel should be displayed?) according to the 3D coordinates on the geometry (i.e. which point is closer to the viewer?). Knowing which points/elements of an object will be rendered into visible pixels allows for more time-consuming calculations for realism such as reflections and textures. Jim Blinn (Utah, Caltech, JPL) introduced environmental mapping (reflection mapping) in 1976. A flat 2D color image is stored and then used to reflect onto a glossy surface. This method was faster than ray tracing. (Ray tracing was derived from ray casting but instead of tracing rays from the viewer's eye to the object to determine hidden surfaces, a ray is drawn from a light source to the object to determine the amount of illumination and/or reflection.)

Blinn also introduced bump mapping in 1978. Since not all surfaces are smooth, bump mapping solved the problem of having to describe wrinkles or bumps by subdividing the geometry so much that there are too many points to calculate efficiently. Instead of changing the geometry, a flat 2D black-and-white image is stored and the image shows where wrinkles or bumps are and how big they are. The surface then reacts to the lighting as if shadows are being caused by wrinkles without changing the geometry. (This is different from displacement mapping, which actually changes the geometry and creates more subdivisions or geometric detail.)

Surface reproduction had become very scientific and the terminology and papers published during this decade include: diffuse reflection, specular reflection, specular highlight, texture mapping, shadow mapping, bump mapping, tile mapping, environment mapping, shadow volumes, z-buffering, scrolling, side-scrolling, and sprites.

By now terminology and concepts were so prevalent and developing so rapidly that the first "bible" of computer graphics was published, *Principles of Interactive Computer Graphics*, written by Bob Sproull (Xerox PARC, Sutherland, Sproull and Asso., Oracle) and William M. Newman (Xerox PARC).

A new kind of moviemaking and new kinds of directors were gaining prominence in the 1970s and their type of movies invited the special effects innovation offered by CGI. This would be the beginning of writing a new formula for the blockbusters that we see today; filled with action, hyper-realism, and special effects. This was also the first decade of filmmakers with a formal education in cinema (called "Film Brats") and who came out of schools like University of Southern California (USC), University of California, Los Angeles (UCLA), and New York University (NYU). Francis Ford Coppola, Martin Scorsese, and George Lucas are examples of this. Steven Spielberg worked his way up over the years as an editor or director on many little-known movies and television shows until getting attention for the TV movie *Duel* (1971) and the hit movie *Jaws* (1975). CGI and special effects would have a prominent place in most of his movies and those of George Lucas. Filmmakers were finding this new technology to be very promising in executing and conveying their unique and modern visions to the world. They were realizing a new type of communication power that computer technology offered and they were becoming ready to harness that power for ultimate authorship.

The traditional movie studios (scions of studios from the Golden Age of Hollywood circa 1920 to 1960) relinquished control over production, finding distribution to be more lucrative. Production would be handed over to independent companies, producers, and/or agents (e.g. Creative Artists Agency, 1975). This resulted in a more "boutique" feeling to production and lower-budget location shooting became the norm. *Rocky* (1976) was an example of this. Distribution got a big boost through video tapes and cable TV at this time (e.g. pay per view and Home Box Office – HBO was founded in 1972). Suddenly access to mass audiences was easier than building theaters and shipping reels of film and this potentially massive national and international audience would need much more entertainment product than ever before.

The 1980s – computer graphics become mainstream

During this decade the number of players involved in CGI increases dramatically. Hollywood studios outsource CGI production allowing the formation of commercial and CGI-dedicated production companies. Big players from the 1970s get bigger and CGI sees more screen time beginning with *Tron* (using 15 minutes of full total CGI animation). The proof of concept that movies could be made completely in CGI (instead of CGI being used for just insert visual effect shots) is shown and the race is on to produce the first completely CGI production with Pixar leading the pack by releasing a series of full CGI animated shorts. During this time Pixar became independent of Lucasfilm (with a little help from Steve Jobs) and was now a CGI production studio. NYIT attempts to produce the first feature-length full CGI movie called "The Works" but it was shelved in 1986. The competition to create the first full CGI movie continued.

However, before the first CGI movie was released, the first CGI/live-action hybrid rock video, *Money for Nothing* (Dire Straits) was aired for MTV Europe in 1987. Animators Ian Pearson and Gavin Blair created the animation on a Quantel Paintbox and would continue on to form the studio Mainframe

Entertainment (currently Rainmaker Studios affiliated with the CGI–animated *Bob the Builder*) to produce the computer-animated TV series, *Reboot* (1990s). Following the popularity of *Money for Nothing*, Digital Productions (John Whitney Jr. and Gary Demos) produced CGI curve characters for the Mick Jagger video *Hard Woman* in 1985. The 1980s rock videos would be remembered for their creative use of 2D animation, stop-motion animation, and graphic effects.

Meanwhile, CGI visual effects advanced rapidly within George Lucas' Lucasfilm new division, Industrial Light & Magic (ILM). ILM was started in 1975 in response to his studio effects needs for the movie, *Star Wars*. During the 1980s, ILM would produce several photo-realistic digital effects including the animated stained-glass knight in *Young Sherlock Holmes* (1985); a morphing woman in *Willow* (1988); the growing planet "Genesis" sequence in *Star Trek II: The Wrath of Khan* (1982); the first 2D digital compositing sequence in *Indiana Jones and the Last Crusade* (1989); and the water pseudopod in *The Abyss* (1989). This period also marks the beginning of ILM's affiliation with many well-known directors including Steven Spielberg, Ron Howard, Francis Ford Coppola, Richard Donner, Robert Zemeckis, Leonard Nimoy, Joe Dante, Mel Brooks, Blake Edwards, Sydney Pollack, James Cameron, and Jim Henson. Over the decades ILM would produce special visual effects for over 300 movies before The Walt Disney Company would acquire them as part of Lucasfilm and the Star Wars franchise in 2012.

However, in the beginning, ILM's success in CGI effects involved other notable persons outside of ILM. Edwin Catmull (Ohio, NYIT, Pixar, Walt Disney Animation Studios) was the first employee and Vice President of Lucasfilm's computer division before moving on to Pixar. Alvy Ray Smith (Stanford, NYIT, Xerox PARC, JPL) also joined ILM with Catmull until he moved to Pixar. John Lasseter, a Walt Disney artist, joined Catmull at ILM also before moving to Pixar where he would oversee all of the animated movies as an executive and receive two Academy awards. (Disney would eventually purchase Pixar in 2006.) Richard Edlund, who worked at ILM on Star Wars left in 1983 to set up his own studio, Boss Film Studio, which transitioned from traditional film effects to CGI effects. They were nominated for Best Visual Effects Academy Award in 1985 for the movie, *2010: The Year We Make Contact* (1984), and also created CGI beer bottles playing football for a series of Budweiser commercials. They continued to work on such popular movies as *Ghostbusters* (1984), *Poltergeist II: The Other Side* (1986), *Tales from the Crypt* (1989), and *Die Hard* (1989).

Other noteworthy computer graphic companies that worked on commercial or movie projects were Information International, Inc. (Triple-I), Mathematical

Applications Group, Inc. (MAGI/Synthavision), Robert Abel and Associates (RA&A), and Digital Effects Inc. (John Whitney Jr. and Gary Demos). These four companies were hired by Disney to work on *Tron*. Additionally, Triple-I was consulted at the beginning of ILM's formation and were known for a short film called *Adam Powers, The Juggler* (1980). It used motion capture of a man juggling and doing back flips. He was not a wireframe model but a rendered skin and clothing character. The short was a sensation at SIGGRAPH 1981. Robert Abel was a designer and founder of RA&A who created TV commercials for companies like 7up and Levi's jeans along with network graphics. His company was credited with the first CGI animated chrome robot in a commercial that aired during Super Bowl XIX. It was called *Brilliance* (1984) and made for the Canned Food Information Council but eventually just became known as the sexy robot commercial. It became a hit because of its human-like motion and reflective surfaces. (Another reflective, liquid mercury chrome-like male robot would take its place in the 1990s and spark the creation of CGI artificial humanoids.)

The early computer graphic companies, like Triple-I, MAGI (Richard Taylor, Bo Gehring, and Larry Elin/Bo Gehring and Associates), RA&A, Evans & Sutherland, Digital Effects, Inc., and Cranston/Csuri, were still using mainframe computers at exorbitant costs. Whitney and Demos were leasing a multimillion-dollar Cray XMP-2 super-computer which was the size of a truck and cost $50,000 for maintenance and $12,000 a month in electricity alone. Additionally, they needed two VAX 1180s to talk to the Cray. With this system Whitney and Demos (Digital Effects, Inc./Digital Productions) created 25 minutes or 300 shots of pure CGI model animation instead of miniatures for all Gunstar spaceships, for planet shots, and high-tech hardware for *The Last Starfighter* in 1984. *Star Wars* (1977) had still used miniature spaceships. Since no one had produced that many CGI special visual effects shots before, 300 shots per movie became the norm for CGI. Whitney and Demos received an Oscar in 1985 for scientific and engineering achievement. However, the cost of industrial computer systems would eventually negatively influence the financial stability of these early companies resulting in buy-outs, poor business decisions, and/or closures.

Former Abel and Associates employees John Hughes, Keith Goldfarb, Charlie Gibson, and Pauline T'so, and Omnibus technical director Larry Weinberg, formed Rhythm and Hues (R&H) in 1987. R&H would specialize in character animation and visual effects for the entertainment industry. They worked on the Mazda Cool World commercials and the Coca Cola Polar Bear campaign. They won many awards for both national and international competitions including the CLIOS, The New York Festivals, the International Monitor Awards, Monte Carlo's Imagina Awards, The Emmy Awards, and two Scientific & Technical Academy Awards. (After working on numerous movies for decades and winning three Academy Awards for Best Visual Effects, including *Life of Pi* in 2012, R&H went bankrupt in 2013.)

While Southern California commercial production and CGI specialty houses were vying for clients (both commercial marketing firms and movie studios) and struggling with the high cost of their hardware, Northern California was making strides of their own. Pacific Data Images (PDI) was a computer production company started in 1980 by Carl Rosendahl and joined by Richard Chuang and Glenn Entis. While Pixar was working on *The Adventures of André and Wally B.* (1984), *Luxo Jr.* (1986), and *Tin Toy* (1988, Oscar award winning), PDI made ten shorts including *Chromosaurus* (1984), which were animated chrome dinosaurs and followed the popularity of bright, shiny, reflective creatures. During the 1980s, they focused on network broadcast graphics for international television shows. They also produced graphics for ABC, CBS, NBC, HBO, Cinemax, MTV, VH1, TNT, and Showtime. They, like other CGI production studios, started out using a mainframe (DEC VAX systems) but were known for introducing the superminicomputer (Ridge 32 computer). Because they were outputting video instead of film, they could use the Sony BVH-2000 to record a frame at a time resulting in a faster and cheaper production process. Their more economic method of production allowed them to stay in business longer and PDI continued to produce hundreds of commercials, contribute special visual effects to at least 70 movies, and produce full CGI-animated movies in conjunction with Dreamworks after signing a co-production deal in 1996 and being purchased in 2000. (Pixar's *Toy Story* was the first fully CGI animated feature in 1995 and PDI/Dreamworks *Antz* was the second in 1998.)

The shift from industrial mainframes to workstations and PCs would open the door for newer players to compete against existing commercial production companies and CGI studios. While video systems, like the Quantel Paintbox, could be faster than available computers at the time, the cost was still prohibitive for most upstarts. Competition in the microcomputer market was forcing standardization in a de facto way. The Control Process/Monitor (CP/M) operating system, the S-100 bus processor/peripheral card, read-only memory (ROM), 5¼ inch floppy drives, Microsoft® Windows®, and Intel processors became the norm. In 1981 IBM entered the microcomputer market making the concept of a PC more respectable. This made it easier for companies to justify purchase and IBM's documentation and recognizable architecture and operating system encouraged the production of thousands of third-party add-in cards and software.

While the IBM PC was still following the design of a generalized computer, there was a concept that CGI required a dedicated type of computer. A graphics workstation was a scaled-down industrialized microcomputer dedicated to processing graphics data. They were designed for technical and scientific use with optimized CPU, graphics quality processing and display, higher memory capacity, and multitasking capability. They could better calculate complex data such as 3D mechanical design, engineering simulation (e.g. computational fluid dynamics), motion animation, faster rendering of images, and include specialized look-up tables (LUTs) and mathematical plots. Workstations might include interfaces such as a multiple high-resolution displays along with a graphics tablet, 3D mice (for manipulating 3D objects), and, of course, a keyboard and a regular mouse.

In 1982, Andy Bechtolsheim and graduate students of Stanford University (SU) designed a computer-aided design (CAD) workstation for the Stanford University Network (SUN). The SUN personal CAD computer was built around the Motorola 68000 with the Unix operating system (open-architecture) with an imbedded frame buffer. Apollo was another early workstation that was developed in 1981 and acquired by Hewlett-Packard (HP) in 1989.

The first company to focus exclusively on 3D modeling computation was Silicon Graphics, Inc. founded by Jim Clark and Marc Hannah of Stanford University in 1981. The early small-sized supercomputers were based on a geometry engine comprised of a very-large-scale integration (VLSI) processor for a geometry pipeline that accelerated calculations needed for 3D processes like matrix transforms, clipping, and scaling operations that provided the transformation to view-space. (The idea of having dedicated hardware for specific performance applications like rendering/Reality Engine™ or a video card/GPU would come up again.) The use of specialized hardware allowed the SGI supercomputers to be an industrial high-end workstation somewhere between the giant mainframes and general-purpose PCs. This made SGI a leader in hardware and software manufacturing for 3D computer graphics that were used in a variety of industries including engineering, science, education, and film production.

Hardware manufacturers saw the benefits of selling software to go with their hardware. This period saw the proliferation of multiple software packages. Animation software was categorized into two types: programmed or interactive. Early animation software was mostly developed as in-house tools by educational institutions or production entities. Usually they were programmed procedures because the people developing them were computer science professionals or engineers. However, as production and CGI studios grew, they took on more artists and needed software that would be interactive so that non-programmers could use it. Interactive processes meant that movement was determined by the animator using keyframes. Artists could move an object and save one position at a time. The computer would then complete or interpolate the in-between positions. This worked for inanimate objects (e.g. vehicles) but expressive characters (people and animals) were difficult to animate this way. Because they have skeletons and joints, they needed to be animated one limb/joint at a time. Since most software was developed in-house for specific purposes, a complete turnkey system that would do everything artists needed for television or movie production did not exist.

Autodesk was founded in 1982 to primarily develop CAD software. Their first program was AutoCAD with the second being AutoFlix for animation in 1986. Eventually, a complete animation system would be released in 1990 called 3D Studio.

Wavefront Technologies was founded in Santa Barbara, California, by Mark Sylvester, Larry Barels, and Bill Kovacs in 1984. The intention was to develop off-the-shelf computer graphics software for television commercials and movies. Personal Visualizer was Wavefront's desktop product released in 1988. CAD users would point-and-click to create high-end photo-realistic rendered images. Co-developed with Silicon Graphics, this product was eventually ported to Sun Microsystems, IBM, HP, Tektronics, DEC, and Sony. Although it was the most turnkey system so far, it was still difficult for artists to use.

Alias Research (Toronto, Canada) was formed in 1983 to make an easy-to-use system for video animation, commercials, and post-production. The software Alias/1 was presented at SIGGRAPH in 1985. Alias/1 and the next version Alias/2 were mostly used in CAD, computer-aided industrial design (CAID), and in entertainment markets. Their list of clients included GM, Timex, Reebok, Oakley, Kenner, BMW, Honda, Volvo, Apple, GE, Motorola, Sony, ILM, Broadway Video, and The Moving Picture Company. Alias 2.4.2 was used in the movie *The Abyss* (1989) running on SGI workstations at ILM.

In 1988 Pixar entered the software business and launched RenderMan which was developed internally but licensed commercially for use by other studios. It would become a mainstay in entertainment CGI production and is still in use today. It was first used on *Tin Toy* in 1988 and has been continually refined and improved over decades. There is the RenderMan shading language, which is a component of the Pixar RenderMan rendering software system. Rendering software communicates between 3D modeling, animation applications (i.e. cameras, geometry, materials, and lights), and the render engine generates high-quality images for display. As of 2015, Pixar RenderMan was available for free for non-commercial purposes. (Today there are numerous proprietary and open source rendering software applications available.)

Photoshop® was released in 1988 by authors Thomas Knoll and John Knoll with developer Adobe® Inc. It would become the industry standard painting and photographic raster graphic editor for digital art in total. It is still widely used today for 2D and 3D image manipulation and enabled Adobe® to become the premiere multinational software manufacturer with several image applications in the Adobe® Creative Suite® of products.

Foreign software developers would also contribute to the modern 3D animation programs still in use today in one form or another. Thomson Digital Image (TDI, France) was a subsidiary of an aircraft simulation company. Their first 3D software Explore was released in 1986. National Film Board of Canada filmmaker Daniel Langlois from Montreal developed Softimage in 1986. Side Effects Software was established in 1987 in Toronto, Canada, by Kim Davidson and Greg Hermanovic, and was based on PRISMS from Omnibus.

During the 1980s the third generation of video game consoles was released by Nintendo and Sega. Atari principals split off to form Activision in 1979 and became a third-party developer for Atari. This was also the golden age of arcade games and had generated $5 billion in 1981. The number of arcades doubled at the beginning of the decade. The video game bubble crashed in 1983 but resurged due to home computers. Some PC owners wrote their own games on Commodore 64s, ZX Spectrums, other IBM PCs or Apple IIs. Bestselling console games included *Super Mario Brothers, Tetris, Pac-Man, The Legend of Zelda, Duck Hunt*, and *Pitfall!*. Jaron Lanier and Thomas G. Zimmerman left Atari in 1985 to form VPL Research, Inc. in the San Francisco Bay area. By 1987 the term "virtual reality" was coined by Jaron Lanier. Interestingly, Lanier and Zimmerman were working on a range of virtual reality gear including a DataGlove, EyePhone head-mounted display, and DataSuit. His company was the first to sell virtual reality goggles (the EyePhone). (In 1999 Sun Microsystems bought VPL's virtual reality and graphics patents.)

The 1980s presented more realistic CGI lighting using global illumination (e.g. ray tracing and radiosity). Photo-realism was also assisted by better shading and rendering procedures thanks to the development of RenderMan and RenderMan shaders. John Turner Whitted was credited with recursive ray tracing, providing an algorithm to simulate global illumination that is still in use today. Soft bounce lighting as seen in interior environments were achieved through radiosity in 1984 by researchers at Cornell and Hiroshima Universities. Simulating ambiguous phenomenon like smoke, water spray, sparks, clouds, fog, snow, dust, meteor tails, stars, galaxies, explosions, fire, stars' abstract visual effects like glowing trails, strands of fur, hair or grass were achieved using particle systems. Particle systems were used in games and CGI using large numbers of sprites (two-dimensional bitmap) or 3D models/objects to create natural phenomena that has no defined borders.

Also useful for the simulation of natural phenomena (e.g. trees, mountains, landscapes, snowflakes) was fractal generating software originated by Benoit Mandelbrot. Fractals are self-simulating elements that when duplicated tend to look like elements found in nature. Many 3D animation programs contain fractal-generating software to create plants. Loren Carpenter (Pixar) was co-inventor of the Reyes rendering algorithm and one of the authors of the PhotoRealistic RenderMan software, which implements Reyes in Pixar movies. He presented *Vol Libre* at SIGGRAPH in 1980, which used fractals to generate a completely CGI landscape. This technique was used to create the fractally landscaped planet for the "genesis effect" scene of *Star Trek II: The Wrath of Khan* (1982).

Other natural animal phenomena like flocking (mass animal movement seen in birds or other animals) was also being proceduralized by Craig W. Reynolds, an artificial life and computer graphics expert who worked on *Tron*. He created a mathematical model of flocking behavior in 1986. Once nature and animal movement began to get proceduralized instead of being animated by hand,

Figure 2.2 Terminator 2: Judgment Day *(1991) behind-the-scenes images courtesy of Stan Winston School of Character Arts.*

Figure 2.3 Terminator 2 *behind-the-scenes images courtesy of Stan Winston School of Character Arts.*

this marked the beginning of hyper-realism. By using principles of nature it becomes possible to apply those principles for fantastic or imaginary entities/environments and make them feel real.

The following Stan Wilson photographs show the use of puppetry and physical effects on the cusp of total reliance upon CGI.

The 1990s: the break-out years, to infinity and beyond!

This decade sees the realization of photo-real CGI. The first full CGI animated feature film, *Toy Story* (1995), is released. Photo-realistic animals are accomplished with the release of *Jurassic Park* (1993) and a hybrid cartoon and realistic mouse character, Stuart Little, becomes the first completely CGI leading character in a movie, blending naturally with live-action actors. *Terminator 2: Judgment Day* (1991) astounds everyone with a believable shape-shifting liquid mercury man. Can synthetic humans and hyper-real humanoids be next?

Advances in animal and human motion help to complete the illusion of life even if realistic treatment of human skin and hair are still in a process of refinement. Motion capture (mocap) had uses beyond entertainment in sports, medicine, robotics, and the military. Special sensors in a suit are attached directly to a performer's body that capture movement and then that animation data is transferred to a digital 3D model. For high-end animation as found in feature films, normally the data is manipulated for improvement. Sometimes, the raw data might be used directly as in video games because the game characters have limited motion (clips) that can be cycled endlessly. The ability to capture gross movements (body) and fine movements (facial) gave animators realistic data to work with thereby improving the believability of CGI characters. However, one primary problem with mocap is how the body moves through space. While the limbs and facial expressions were captured, the entire body's physical position in 3D space was not. Most importantly, the performer's feet did not appear to be in contact with the floor and would slide. Therefore, a system was needed to accurately move objects as they traveled in space.

Match moving (motion tracking, camera tracking) uses identifiable features on an object to lock onto and follow the object as it moves through space. The motion path data is then transferred to a digital object. The same principle can be applied to camera motion so that a physical moving camera's motion data can be applied to a virtual camera. The virtual camera can then move through a virtual set or environment allowing elements (like people) in the live environment to be copied (composited) to the virtual environment (like the CGI Gotham City shots in *Batman Forever*, 1995) or to allow CGI elements to be placed in the live environment (as in *Death Becomes Her*, 1992, and *Jurassic Park*, 1993).

Flocking and herding were used for more than animals. *Titanic* (1997) had CGI crowds and CGI stunt people. Also *Titanic* had the first photo-realistic water and vapor. CGI for natural phenomena was becoming undetectable as with the CGI tornadoes in *Twister* (1996).

With so many corporations using computer technology, schools started creating CGI programs by the hundreds catering to the high-profile use of CGI in entertainment and students looking for an artistic career. Universities, community colleges, and technical trade schools partnered with hardware and software companies to teach their systems. Most students would get entry-level jobs in the boutique studios. At the more successful and prestigious schools, students were recruited before graduation with only an operational understanding of one 3D software application. In California, State schools were encouraged by industry to teach software packages to supply the studios with as many digital artists as possible. (Additionally, this practice had the effect of lowering wages by increasing the number of available digital workers who were once scarce at the beginning of the decade.) CGI training became training in software tools and less of a comprehensive art/design education.

The transition from traditional film workers to digital film workers was disruptive to the entire movie industry and was a factor in changing Hollywood movies to the mega-million-dollar blockbusters of today. Traditional Hollywood movie studios were once union shops that had formed during a worldwide transition to the industrial age. The golden age of motion pictures started around the beginning of the 20th century. During that time, traditional movie workers came out of a guild-like process involving apprenticeship. Later, higher-level film workers (technicians, directors, producers) were formally educated from colleges and universities. Computer graphic workers replaced many of these more traditional film workers, especially artists and technicians, and they tended to not be represented by unions. So, wages and job roles could fluctuate, and workers could be interchangeable. Additionally, digital work is mostly desk work so the romanticized image of the movie studio with sets, a backlot, costuming, props, esoteric equipment created solely for the motion picture industry with obscure and mysterious jobs that were difficult to fill was changing to resemble a more corporate image of office cubicles with rows of computer-covered desks. The reason most filmmakers were attracted to the medium was because of the artistic autonomy offered during pre-production, stage/location production, and post-production. These tended to be unfamiliar areas to executives. However, as pre-production, production, and post-production lines blurred and creative decisions could be made in an office viewing a computer screen, this allowed more corporate executive involvement (or interference) leading to a committee-like decision-making process as opposed to the auteur process of previous times.

Operating out of a corporate environment allowed the studios to decentralize from Hollywood and they merged, grew, and developed into or with computer/software manufacturers, television networks, boutique special effects companies, CGI production companies, and even entered the video game industry. Digital workers upset the status quo. Movie jobs that were once highly specialized, and unusual (like optical printing, animation/rostrum camera operation, 2D animation painting, 2D rotoscoping, film color correction, still photography, cinematography, editing, visual effects), could be replaced by a desk worker with a computer and the right software. Since just about anyone could be trained to operate a computer running software, human resource departments changed to manage mass layoffs, replacement of employees, and manage studio training in response to restructuring and re-tooling during the transition from traditional movie workers to digital workers. Computer graphics made it easier for executives and investors to monitor production and make financial decisions. So, computer graphics was a major factor in allowing the movie industry to grow from being centralized in the US to becoming large multinational conglomerates, like any other corporation.

Thus, moviemaking became more like software development using the Agile production management method characterized by division of tasks into chunks of work (requiring more specialized yet replaceable people with diminished authorship) and frequent reassessment, revisions, and newly adapted plans. This marked the end of the old Hollywood production process and the beginning of a new corporate digital production assembly pipeline (a sample pipeline was covered in *Filming the Fantastic: A Guide to Visual Effects Cinematography*, 2nd edition, 2011).

An example of how movie studios were starting to operate more like software manufacturers is when SGI was very busy teaming up with ILM as a graphics lab and with Dreamworks to make entertainment products. They also acquired Alias Research and Wavefront Technologies putting them in the software business in addition to being a leading workstation manufacturer. Prior to this, Microsoft had acquired Canadian software company Softimage putting PCs in the 3D software business. Maya® 3D software (produced by Alias Systems Corporation) was released in 1998 and ZBrush (by Pixologic in 1999) sculpting software would transform human and creature artistry and character development, directly contributing to the astounding photo-real/hyper-realistic sculpted characters that would be a signature of the millennium.

PCs started to rival workstations due to improved microprocessor performance. By the second half of the 1990s, Intel processors gave way to Pentium, Celeron, and Dual and Quad Core processors, allowing for better graphics for 3D and games. In the mid-1990s the game engine concept is invented. In the 1980s game codes were written from the bottom up for each game and fairly disposed of when creating a new game, which started from scratch all over again. With the popularity of the first-person shooter (FPS) games, game developers could license core parts of software (like the game logic algorithm, rendering engine, audio engine, physics engine, collision detection, and artificial intelligence) and create their own game assets (characters, graphics, levels, weapons, etc.) for modification ("modding") of the game. Licensing software became a lucrative source of revenue for game developers outside of consumer sales and contributed to the proliferation of FPS games which were spinoffs or third-party developments of *Doom* and *Quake*. The Unreal® Engine (1998) would become one of the most widely used game engines.

The introduction of reusable game engines led to modification for specific uses outside of entertainment and started the gamification of information. Serious games were created for use in medical, science, education, military simulation, visualization, and training. The CryEngine (2002) is one example of this. Developments in CGI directly influenced the game industry by allowing more developers to create game assets and engines with more realism and dynamism.

PC gaming in combination with the Internet saw the first Multi-User Dungeon (MUD) leading to the first massively multiplayer online role-playing games (MMORPGs) into the mass market. The merging of games and moviemaking comes in the form of the first machinima (machine and cinema) video, *Diary of a Camper* (1996). Using the graphics engine from the game *Quake*, the game would be played in real-time, recorded and edited together to tell a story. This is faster than theatrical CGI production, which is not produced live, but rendered, recorded or filmed and edited offline in non-real time. Games are played in real-time and are, therefore, immediate.

Consoles (fifth generation like Sega Saturn (1994), PlayStation (1994), and the Nintendo 64 (1996)) competed by transitioning from 2D to 3D graphics and the first games on mobile phones were released. Handheld portables like the Nintendo Game Boy, Sega Game Gear and Atari Lynx proliferated with the Game Boy being the most popular and long lasting. Sega announced a VR headset for the Sega Genesis console at the Consumer Electronics Show in 1993. Arcades, too, tried to compete by introducing more immersive virtual-reality experiences. In 1991, the Virtuality Group launched a series of VR arcade games and devices like goggles and real-time imagery with stereoscopic 3D immersive environments. Some units were networked together for multiplayer experiences although you would have to be in the same room/building. (The first movie to show the concept of VR was released in 1992, *The Lawnmower Man*, and was loosely based on Jaron Lanier and his VPL research lab.)

Tim Berners-Lee, an English engineer and computer scientist, had invented the world wide web in 1989 and he executed the first communication between a client and a server. He created the first web browser and website. He is the founder of the World Wide Web Foundation and the director of the World Wide Web Consortium (W3C), which guides continued development. By the end of the decade the term Wi-Fi is invented when users connect to the Internet without wires.

CGI rendering improvements are the cause of increased realism but CGI is a calculation-hungry beast. According to Jim Blinn (Utah, JPL) rendering time remains constant because no matter how fast computers become, better quality and innovation will always be demanded. The people who use CGI will never use less time to do the same thing no matter how fast or efficient hardware/software becomes. This is called Blinn's Law. For *Toy Story*, Pixar went from 53 to 300 processors with one frame of film taking from 7 to 15 hours to render or process.

It is during this decade that the term "render farm" is coined with CGI production requiring rooms of networked computers configured to run in parallel and with input and output managed by a queue. At first render farms were localized within the production environment but eventually advances in Internet speed and fiber optic cables would allow the use of remote render farms provided by entities possessing massive computing power (like universities) and willing to collect a per project fee leading to a new type of business opportunity. (The term Internet "cloud" had not been invented yet.)

While theatrical movie CGI was processing imagery offline and in parallel processes, television (similar to video games) needed immediate effects and environments that would work with live broadcasters. Much the way the weatherman/woman is instantly composited against a 2D weather graphic using blue or green screen and chroma keying, it was necessary to create a 3D environment to put announcers in. In 1991, the Japanese broadcasting corporation, NHK, created the first synthetic virtual set or studio called Synthevision. For the virtual set, camera tracking was used so that as the real camera moves on the announcer, changes in the virtual set match the camera angle, focal length, and/or perspective. Much later, as we will see, the virtual set/studio will eventually become the virtual backlot for use in movies and will mean something slightly different.

The decade ends with the release of *The Matrix* (1999) written and directed by the Wachowskis. It had a major cultural impact, created a new sci-fi movie subgenre (cyberpunk), and showed that CGI was capable of creating photo-realistic hyper-real virtual worlds expressive of advanced metaphysical concepts. By this time computer technology had become a metaphor for human consciousness and was more accepted than the analogy made in *Tron*. The extensive use of photographic texture mapping to create virtual digital urban environments did not stop with any one special effect method. The seamlessly integrated use of a variety of techniques, including bullet-time (which was invented for commercials, e.g. Smirnoff, 1996), opened a world of futuristic high-concept subject matter capable of making the abstract tangible and action-packed. In addition to virtual environments, there were CGI bio-mechanical Sentinels, airborne martial arts fighting (wire removal), camera tracking, spatial/temporal manipulation, and the innovative use of capturing facial details to be recombined and edited later. The idea of digitizing all photographic data for later manipulation is used today as digital libraries have become valuable studio commodities. *The Matrix* won four Academy Awards for Visual Effects, Sound, Editing, and Sound Effects. It would become a franchise consisting of two sequels, comic books, video games and animation shorts. The Wachowskis were influenced by Japanese manga and anime, *Ghost in the Shell* (1995), and comic book/graphic novel treatments would continue to contribute to entertainment franchises and blockbuster formulae over the next decades.

The 2000s – computer graphics become a global business

During the millennium movies, entertainment in general, and especially CGI, became big business. Effects budgets grew, mergers and acquisitions proliferated, and Hollywood became a mixture of multinational conglomerates and Wall Street commodities. Movie franchises were born of sequels and included theatrical releases; games; DVDs; pay-per-view; domestic and foreign TV licensing and distribution; in-flight screening; toys; product placement; amusement parks; and profit sharing/royalties that could last for the lifetime of the franchise and beyond. CGI effects are no longer a small component of movies but an expected fundamental that should be integral to box office success. By this time mostly all big budget movies contain large amounts of digital or CGI elements whether recognized or not. Seamless integration prevents most people from recognizing how much of the footage is altered or virtual. The cost of making movies increases and, like Blinn's Law of ever-growing rendering need, Parkinson's Law states that the film budget will always expand to fully meet the capital available regardless of product quality. And that capital was available in the form of other people's money, especially outside investors, Wall Street hedge funds and big investment banks (Lehman Brothers and Goldman Sachs). Much like the way mortgages were bundled into securities at this time and sold off in tranches (slices), studio movies were bundled into securities and sold off in portions called slates to investors. Studios could spend less of their own money while still reaping distribution fees off the top. Additionally, studios started using social media to market movies as marketing is still one of the primary expenses of the entertainment industry.

At this time the major Hollywood studios consist of Time Warner, 20th Century Fox, Viacom, Sony, Walt Disney, and NBC Universal. Independent production companies and independent subsidiaries (indies) like Warner's New Line, Fox's Searchlight, and NBC Universal's Focus Feature (among many others) might be contracted to produce films for the studios. By not being consumed with movie production, the studios could focus on the business of movies and the making of the deal. In 2000, AOL purchased Time Warner for an estimated $182 billion. This was the most expensive buyout in US history. This merger/buyout resulted in a global media/entertainment conglomerate consisting of Internet services, Netscape browser, Warner Brothers studio, Cable News Network (CNN), and Time publishing.

In 2005 Viacom's Paramount Pictures acquired Dreamworks studio for $1.6 billion which was started in 1994 by Steven Spielberg, Jeffrey Katzenberg, and David Geffen. Disney acquired Miramax for $80 million in 1993 and previous owners Harvey and Bob Weinstein founded the Weinstein Company in 2005. The Walt Disney Company purchased Marvel Entertainment for

$4 billion in 2009. Disney also purchased Pixar for an estimated $7.4 billion in 2006, which made Steve Jobs Disney's largest shareholder. Combining production, marketing, and streaming/pay-per-view Internet distribution like Netflix, Apple TV+, and Amazon Prime, Disney launched Disney+ in 2019.

Many of the major franchises that started before or during the 2000s would continue throughout the millennium. Prominent series are X-Men; The Lord of the Rings; Shrek; Toy Story; Harry Potter; The Fast and The Furious; Spider Man; Bourne; Pirates of the Caribbean; Chronicles of Narnia; Mission Impossible; The Mummy; Indiana Jones; Star Trek; Star Wars; Batman; The Matrix; The Terminator; Alien; Transformers; Planet of the Apes; Superman, Die Hard; James Bond; Hannibal; Friday the 13th; and Halloween.

The Pixar/Disney relationship yielded the most movies yet to come out of Pixar including *Monsters Inc.*; *Finding Nemo*; *The Incredibles*; *Cars*; *Ratatouille*; *WALL-E*; and *Up*. Parent studios started their own animation CGI companies to make feature animated films and/or franchises like Cloudy with a Chance of Meatballs (Columbia Pictures/Sony Pictures Animation, 2009); Ice Age franchise (Blue Sky Studios, 20th Century Fox); Despicable Me franchise (Illumination, Universal Pictures, 2010); How to Train Your Dragon franchise (DreamWorks Animation, Paramount Pictures, 2010); Open Season franchise (Sony Pictures Animation, Columbia Pictures, 2006); Happy Feet franchise (Animal Logic, Village Roadshow Pictures, Warner Bros. Pictures, 2006); Surf's Up (Sony Pictures Animation, Columbia Pictures, 2007); Beowulf (ImageMovers, Shangri-La Entertainment, Paramount Pictures, Warner Bros. Pictures, 2007); Kung Fu Panda (DreamWorks Animation, Paramount Pictures, 2008); Monsters vs Aliens (DreamWorks Animation, Paramount Pictures, 2009); Shark Tale (Dreamworks Animation, Dreamworks Pictures, 2004); The Polar Express (Imagemovers, Warner Bros. Pictures, 2004); Megamind (DreamWorks Animation, Pacific Data Images, Paramount Pictures, 2010); Meet the Robinsons (2007), Bolt (2008), and Tangled (2010) (Walt Disney Animation Studios, Walt Disney Pictures); among many others. Modern CGI capabilities allowed for the remaking of movies that had before been accomplished with makeup or other traditional effects like *Planet of the Apes*, *King Kong*, *E.T.: The Extra-Terrestrial*, and *Star Wars: The Special Edition*.

The push to create 100% believable CGI humans was almost realized in the movie adaptation of the video game, *Final Fantasy: The Spirits Within* (Square Pictures, Columbia Pictures, 2001) with CGI characters. The most complete character was a female, Dr. Aki Ross. Although the characters were close in appearance to photo-real live-action humans, their performance was lacking and the ambivalent reaction to them was linked to the concept of the "uncanny valley," which suggests that depictions of humans that are close to recognizable but not exactly the same as humans can elicit feelings of repulsion. The gap in human depiction exists between completely stylized people (like animation) and living people. Within that recognizability gap are figures, like humanoid robots, life-sized dolls, and corpses, that are uncannily familiar yet eerily dissimilar to live humans. Likewise, the Tom Hanks character in *The Polar Express* (2004) and the characters in *Beowulf* (2007) and *A Christmas Carol* (2009) elicited an "uncanny valley" reaction. However, when synthespians and virtual stuntmen were displayed with limited screen time, their acceptance was more guaranteed because scrutiny was reduced, and they were in constant motion. (A synthespian is a computer rendition of an actor and is a blending of the words synthetic with thespian. Jeff Kleiser and Diana Walczak of the Kleiser-Walczak Construction Co. coined the term "synthespian" in 1987 or 1988.)

Motion, therefore, became an equal measurement to visual accuracy in human CGI duplication. Although not strictly adhering to "normal" human proportions and appearance, the Gollum character in *The Lord of the Rings: The Fellowship of the Ring* (Weta Digital, 2001) marked the advancement from mocap to performance capture. Motion capture has a long history being used for traditional 2D animation when people or animals were captured on film and traced or rotoscoped to lend realism to cartoon characters. Later when combined with motion tracking and the use of sensors or markers, full figure data could be transferred to CGI characters. However, full figure motion was not enough to convincingly duplicate humans. Subtle motion in smaller muscle groups like the face and hands are important visual cues people instinctively look for in expression and emotions.

At this time there was the realization that for a CGI character to be life-like it had to be imbued with the entirety of an actor's performance (Andy Serkis who gave validity to the concept of mocap performance acting), which was achieved through pain-staking mocap, motion tracking, facial capture, and skilled animation editing by numerous digital animators. In addition to the Gollum performance, creating a near-naked humanoid required using anatomical advances like subsurface scattering (skin translucency), muscle systems (muscle contraction/expansion and volume below the skin), skinning systems (skin wrinkling and reacting to muscle and bone movement), facial animation system, physical imperfections (cuts, scars, blemishes), eye detail/layering and reactions, and attention to details like pores, body and eye moisture, facial and body hair.

Artificial intelligence in the form of cloth, rigid body (stretch and squash deformation), and crowd simulation could free animators to focus on actor performance. Massive (Multiple Agent Simulation System in Virtual Environment) was software developed in New Zealand for The Lord of the Rings battle scenes. The software controls each soldier's reaction and actions by switching and blending pre-recorded motion clips. The pre-programed crowd behavior ranges from merely walking around and talking to stadium crowd and mayhem behavior. Massive was licensed for use on other movie productions such as *Rise of the Planet of the Apes* and *Avatar*. *The Fellowship of the Ring* won four Academy Awards for Cinematography, Visual Effects, Makeup, and Original Score.

The Curious Case of Benjamin Button (2008) required realistic character depiction of a man aging in reverse for over 45 years without heavy reliance upon traditional prosthetic makeup and with skeletal changes throughout. Digital Domain used a variety of effects and a new procedure called emotion capture to transfer Brad Pitt's performance onto several CGI heads. It was a complicated process, which mainly consisted of creating a library of Brad Pitt facial expressions, using full body computer scans of Pitt to create three figures of him in his 80s, 70s, and 60s, using various body actors with blue hoods whose heads would be replaced by CGI, and matching CGI data to Pitt's performances. The film was nominated for 13 Academy Awards and won three for Art Direction, Makeup, and Visual Effects.

Towards the end of the decade in 2009 the Avatar franchise started (James Cameron, Lightstorm Entertainment, Dune Entertainment, Ingenious Film Partners, Distributed by 20th Century Fox) as part of the big budget blockbuster productions costing $200 million plus. It surpassed Cameron's *Titanic* as the highest grossing film at the time bringing in at least $2 billion at the box office. At the time of writing, sequels to the original *Avatar* are scheduled for release (as of the time of writing) in 2021, 2023, 2025, and 2027. The production of *Avatar* introduced new technology and a new approach to filmmaking. Most importantly, the movie merged CGI-animated mocap with a virtual camera system, borrowing from 3D video games, that would allow the director to see the CGI characters while looking at the live actors in mocap capture. The actors wore mocap suits for gross body movement capture along with small facial cameras that recorded all their expressions and eye movement while performing. When CGI interacts with live action, a simulcam was used so that the director could see the live action transferred to the CGI characters and merged in the virtual environment or augmented reality simultaneously. Normally, live and CGI were kept separate until merged in a post-production process, but by being able to view both together during filming, the acting, camera, and directorial decisions could be made in real time without waiting for resulting composites.

The amount of data that needed to be stored and made accessible to everyone involved in the production globally, from Weta in New Zealand to ILM in the US, required a new cloud computing and digital management system called Gaia, created by Microsoft for *Avatar*. Weta's render farm used 35,000 core processors and 4,000 Hewlett-Packard servers, 104 terabytes of RAM and three petabytes of network storage. Each minute of the final film took approximately 17 gigabytes of storage.

The 2010s – undetectable from reality

The creation of full CGI movies in the form of feature animation proved the concept that movies could be produced entirely within the computer. *Avatar* also proved the concept that live-action movies could use CGI characters and environments produced with real-time assistance from game technology, video/digital cameras, and mocap/motion tracking for live compositing and directorial control during production. If production and post-production could be completely digital, why not pre-production? Using CGI animation processes, live-action movies could be planned and animated completely in the computer with synthesized cameras, locations, and actors as a type of animated storyboard (previsualization, previs, previz). It was now possible for live-action movies to be completely digital from script to screen including pre-production, production, post-production and distribution. Live action could now benefit from the same processes used by feature animation. This capability would allow even more players to enter the movie production business and increase the amount of content like never before.

In the 1990s digital cameras started to enter motion picture cinematography creating digital cinematography. Although electronic cinematography had existed in the form of video cameras based on the cathode-ray tube for television broadcast since the 1930s, video cameras were used for immediacy and not considered to be equal to the picture quality of film. However, from the 1980s and onward, companies like Sony and Kodak were developing high-definition professional cameras and marketing them to still photographers. Movie cameras based on the charge-coupled device (CCD) image sensor technology for image capture (originally for military and scientific use) resulted in images made of pixels (picture elements) and are considered to be of high image quality when the pixel count is in the thousands. Early digital movie cameras had 2,000 horizontal pixels and advanced to have 4,000 horizontal pixels. Arguably, the pixel count decision is based on what image quality best matches the theatrical release standard of 35mm film (although special release formats like 70 mm and Vistavision may factor into the decision). Today 4K cameras are widely used.

Likewise, most theaters no longer project film. Digital projectors receive movies via the Internet, hard drives or satellite networks in 2K or 4K. A joint venture between the major studios, Digital Cinema Initiatives, LLC, established standards for digital projection starting in 2005. Digital projection is convenient for distribution allowing the distributor to readily control content (trailers and advertisements) and theater selection and scheduling. It also allows transition to a home market when including consumers who have high-definition access through their home theater system resulting in increased ticketing, rental, purchase, and profit.

Much like the process of making a CGI feature animation movie, previs creates the entire live-action movie in the computer before ever recording the main actors. Low resolution avatar-like characters stand in for the actors and dialog, effects, locations, and sound may be included so that the full movie can be timed out just as the final picture would be. This is where all the creative decisions are made fairly inexpensively so that production time and budget can be made more efficient. All the planning-intensive aspects of blockbuster moviemaking like stunts, special effects, fight scenes, and conceptualizations are completed at this stage before production starts. (However, a complete digital moviemaking process does not mean that development, pre-production, production, post-production, and distribution are executed linearly. Additionally, many movies are shot in stereoscopic 3D, which adds more data into the process. Often these stages are executed in parallel and this has resulted in new production management procedures and tools with numerous production management software manufacturers and services.)

The total digital process of today's moviemaking empowers principles like the director, cinematographer, CG lighting supervisor, producers, and other executive participants to conceptualize, design the look and feel of the movie, and control production in ways unavailable in the past. A look at the workflow of *Gravity* (2013) from the November 2013 *American Cinematographer* magazine outlines 14 stages including orbit trajectory design; previs (low-res animated version of the movie); CG pre-lighting for each sequence of the movie; pre-color timing for the release versions of the movie; camera movement trajectories and lighting for the point-of-view of each character; live-action lighting with motion control; live-action zero-gravity puppeteering; live-action photography of the space capsule interiors; animating, modeling and lighting the photographed shots; compositing the live-action shots and the CG elements; color timing of individual elements; color timing for the high-definition master version of the movie; converting the movie to stereoscopic 3D; and final color grading for 3D white screen and 3D Imax release.

This process is illustrative of most of today's blockbuster movies in which almost everything is CGI including characters, character costume design, locations, set design, effects, animals, lighting, mocap, cameras, and props. The actors are usually photographed in a green-screen set or minimally furnished set. This means that asset management or all the CG elements are stored and manipulated in a cloud environment that can be assessed by those involved creatively and technically and be production managed and tracked by those involved in organization and scheduling. Also, all of the participants could be scattered globally thereby increasing coordination complexity. (CG assets are valuable because they can be reused and repurposed for future projects/sequels or licensed to others creating a "virtual backlot" of data. Therefore, storage and library cataloging is important.)

Previs (previsualization) companies were established to service the movie franchise blockbuster industry, with the most notable being The Third Floor, Inc. (formed 2004, e.g. *Mission Impossible* credit), Proof (formed 2002, e.g. *Guardian of the Galaxy*), Halon entertainment (formed 2003, e.g. *World War Z*), and Argon Effects (c. 2012, e.g. *Alien: Covenant*). One of the largest previs companies, The Third Floor, with facilities in Los Angeles, London, Canada, and Australia, began doing previs for George Lucas on *Star Wars: Episode III* on Skywalker Ranch (from which the company name is derived) and, since then, has worked on several movies, television series, commercials, games, theme attractions, and VR. In 2019 The Third Floor launched an original content initiative called Story Attic. The purpose is to showcase their artists' work and develop original content.

As previs grew to encapsulate areas of development, pre-production, production, post-production, and release, The Third Floor and CEO, Chris Edwards, collaborated with the entertainment industry to create a term that would better explain how a multidisciplinary, multimedia, and transmedia worldbuilding approach works. The working definition of "virtual production"

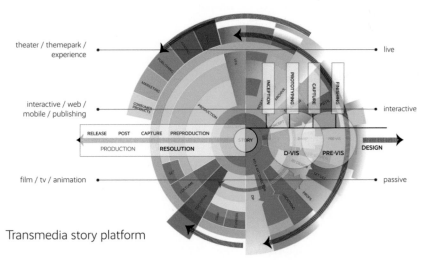

Figure 2.4 *Mandala for non-linear virtual production,* © *Alex McDowell, 2004. Courtesy of Alex McDowell, Director, World Building Media Lab.*

is "a collaborative and interactive digital filmmaking process, which begins with virtual design and digital asset development and continues in an iterative, nonlinear process throughout the production" (*The VES Handbook of Visual Effects: Industry Standard VFX Practices and Procedures*, 2nd edition, edited by J.A. Okun and S. Zwerman, Focal Press, 2014). As previs developed into virtual production, designer Alex McDowell created a graphic that attempted to capture all the areas in which digital design and execution is involved in any given product and series of products.

Predominantly computer- and cloud-based production encouraged new players to start their own streaming or production facility (ancillary to the established big studios) or their own movie/television studio (competition to the established big studios). Netflix (1998) started out as a monthly mail subscription-based DVD sales and rental company. By the 2000s Internet speed, bandwidth, and costs had improved to accommodate movie streaming so they increased their library and introduced a movie recommendation algorithm based on customer ratings. In 2011, DreamWorks Animation SKG, Inc. signed a deal to distribute its movies through Netflix. In 2013 DreamWorks and Netflix co-produced a web TV series, *Turbo Fast*.

Since then Netflix has become an original producer of movie and television content. As a distributor it has many exclusive pay TV deals with several studios and some game manufacturers and has subscribers worldwide. At the time of writing, Netflix showed 300 original content titles worldwide (content financed by Netflix and exclusively distributed by Netflix including movies and television programs) in 2017 and received 23 Primetime Emmy awards in 2018. It had 250 million video-on-demand subscribers worldwide in 2018 with approximately 60 million of those in the US. Netflix's original content was produced outside Netflix but in 2018, Netflix purchased a movie studio in Albuquerque, New Mexico. At $6.3 billion in 2017, Netflix spent more on original and acquired content than other Internet companies like Amazon, Hulu, Apple, and Facebook, and was approaching the spending of traditional networks, like Disney, Time Warner, Fox, and NBCU.

Online retailer, Amazon, which is a close competitor to Netflix, created Amazon Prime, an annual subscription service that included free shipping to members along with discounts on Kindle books and streaming video-on-demand in 2006. In 2013, it distributed its own original content through the Prime video service with some projects produced by Amazon Studios (2010). They produced 23 original title series in 2017 and have 26 million Prime subscribers in the US. Hulu, Apple iTunes, Sling TV, Roku, YouTube, Google, and others joined the streaming subscription business as consumers were cutting their expensive cable packages that included cable stations like HBO and Showtime, etc.

Not to be outdone by Netflix, Disney merged with 21st Century Fox in 2019 to produce its own subscription streaming service called Disney +, to distribute its own content. Having already acquired the Marvel and Star Wars franchises, Disney now had Fox's X-Men, Alien, The Fantastic Four, Avatar and Predator movie franchises in addition to television shows like *The Simpsons*, *Family Guy*, *Modern Family*, *How I Met Your Mother* and *The X-Files*. Fox also had its own movie studio, the National Geographic channel, Asian and European channels or networks, 30% of Hulu, and numerous regional sports networks.

As the big studios reduced their production of original material (because it was considered too risky) in favor of sequels, prequels, and spinoffs within franchises, non-traditional studios (e.g. Netflix, Amazon) stepped up to fill the void. The 2010s would be known as the decade of the franchises (including both successes and flops). The most successful franchises include Harry Potter, Planet of the Apes, Transformers, Twilight, The Hangover, Pirates of the Caribbean, Fast Five, Mission Impossible, Cars, Sherlock Holmes, Thor, and Captain America. This decade would also be known as the time when comic books were king. The Marvel Universe alone released 20 movies, the X-Men released seven movies, and the Spiderman franchise released four movies. The DC Universe was less prolific with seven releases. Pixar led the animation franchises with 10 releases, and Illumination (Despicable Me franchise) had four releases. In total there have been about 418 CGI-animated movies released from a variety of studios/producers from 1995 to 2019 (with some to be released after 2019) compared to about 151 2D traditional feature-animated movies made from 1960 to 1989 worldwide.

New virtual production players, decentralization of visualization facilities, cloud-based connectivity, and remote managerial tools and practices grew the number of professionals, artists, and technicians involved in transmedia productions. An examination of movie digital crew members and outsource companies can provide a glimpse into how hundreds of millions of dollars are spent on digital production compared to the 1980s and 1990s. While it is outside the scope of this chapter to give an in-depth analysis of movie credits, suffice to say that there is much overlap now between traditional non-digital work and pure digital work. Because past non-digital creative areas such as camera, set design, costume design, makeup, stunts, editing, sound, and art department now use some form of digital tools and/or storage/manipulation, it would take a much longer time to examine and sift the digital workers from the non-digital workers. Even special effects, which is the term mostly used to describe physical effects including model making, puppetry, and physical explosives/pyrotechnics (and might be integrated in stunt work) today rely on some form of digital tools/manipulation in some aspect of their process, if only in planning. (Visual effects usually refer to the use of in-camera, special photographic effects, post-production, or digital effects.)

Therefore, using publicly available movie data (IMDb.com) and using the same categories within feature animation (visual effects, camera and electrical, animation) and the same categories within live-action movies (visual effects, animation), an attempt was made to provide some consistency in definitions and use of digital tools. Using categories is a shorthand way to differentiate digital workers from non-digital workers although there is a caveat for the basis of making such a gross assumption. Another caveat to mention regarding digital worker headcount is to avoid the assumption that these numbers are finite to production or studio. Studios often have multiple productions in progress simultaneously and workers may be dedicated to one production or may transfer between various productions as needed. Also the same category may be completely different according to entertainment venue (e.g. camera and electrical was added to feature animation because many times cameras are virtual in this type or production. Although movie cameras are digital, the camera category was left out of the live-action movie comparison because it could not be known at a superficial glance how the camera data was being used.) While this is a quick approximation of the growth of digital crews per movie project, there are some superficial generalizations to be gleaned.

The following graphs were compiled from cast and crew lists and the use of other outside companies used in production of three Pixar Toy Story series (from 1995 to 2019) and five live-action movies showing digital crew progression of milestone movies from the Tron, Jurassic Park, and The Avengers series from (1982 to 2019).

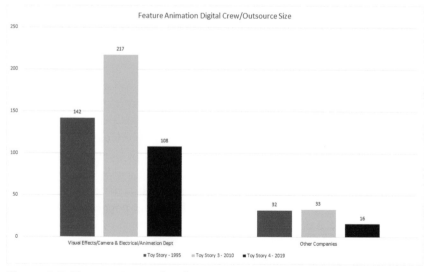

Figure 2.5 *Feature animation digital crew/outsource size.*

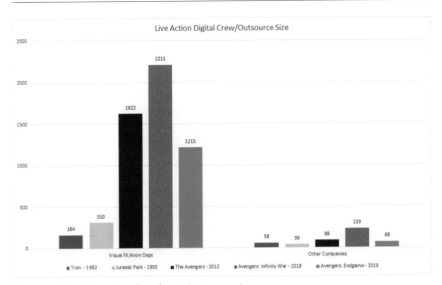

Figure 2.6 *Live-action digital crew/outsource size.*

Pixar/Disney used a peak number of 217 visual effects, camera, and animation workers on *Toy Story 3* in 2010. They outsourced or used at least 33 different outside companies. When Disney purchased Pixar in 2006, this may have affected the growth in personnel. However, it is interesting to note that by 2019 the number of digital workers decreased far below the count for the first *Toy Story* in 1995. There may be a variety of reasons for this not the least of which could be the accumulation of a data library resulting in less original modeling/animation/lighting. Also the experience of producing so many movies by 2019 may have resulted in an infrastructure and procedural streamlining that required fewer participants to execute similar looking content. Also, by their nature, feature animation companies are very self-contained with a long history of refining the production workflow and pipeline. This has enabled them to increase image and storytelling quality while maintaining more managerial control over scheduling, budget, and personnel. (Pixar offered a public pipeline management tool called Universal Scene Description or USD starting in 2016. Take a look at the document for USD on the Pixar website to learn more about the type of pipeline used in CG animation.)

Live-action movies, being much more complicated than a self-contained feature animation project, should take longer to reach the same semblance of control that animation enjoys. A cursory look at the change in digital workers based on film credits. From *Tron* (1982) to *Jurassic Park* (1993) there was a growth in workers of 89.02%. From *Jurassic Park* (1993) to *The Avengers* (2012) there was a whopping increase in workers of 423.23%. From *The Avengers* (2012) to *Avengers: Infinity War* (2018) workers only increased 36.31%. Finally, from *Avengers: Infinity War* (2018) to *Avengers: Endgame* (2019) there was actually a decrease in workers of 45.05%. These numbers show a tapering off of digital workers from 2012 to 2019. The reasons for a tapering off of workers from 2012 to 2019 might be numerous. Like the reasons above for Pixar/Disney, the reuse/repurposing of data libraries might save time and money reducing original content creation. The Avengers franchise may have access to all the other data created for its multitude of sequels, prequels, and spinoffs. The cumulative experience of all the prior participants is also an efficiency factor.

Altogether, this perfunctory look at select feature animation and live-action movies over the years resembles a bell curve used to describe the technology life cycle. We have already passed through the emergent hype cycle of CGI in which expectations and realities were divergent, on to early adoption, then to mass adoption and use during the market-growth period and we are now in the longer-term, elastic, expanding, mature market. As a technology matures it plateaus until a market decline or the next innovative trend starts the process all over again.

A topic for further study could be an analysis of the continuing need for thousands of digital workers and their origins and prospects for future work. It is yet to be seen how their skill sets will transfer to the newest medium of virtual reality, but it is highly likely that the multidisciplinary and transmedia virtual production process used today has laid a fertile foundation for expansion into VR production on various levels for diverse usage as we travel into the next hype cycle. (See Chapter 12.)

Chapter 3
Performance capture

Throughout fantasy film history unique characters and creatures were brought to life through makeup, puppetry of scaled or full-size creations, stop-motion animation, or drawn animation. Today we use a variety of methods to capture the performance of the puppeteer and actor to animate computer graphic characters. This recorded performance can then be edited and enhanced by skilled animators. Over the years there have been many books and schools that have taught artists how to create digital sets and characters. This knowledge has become so widespread that many talented creators offer a wide assortment of these prebuilt assets online at sites such as www.turbosquid.com. Since digital puppets are now readily available to the filmmaker this chapter will relate how we capture the human element to bring life to our store-bought characters.

The following will outline the set-up of the Qualysis motion-capture system for entertainment purposes. From their website in the "About" section:

> With offices in Europe, North America and Asia and with a global network of dis-
> tributors and partners, Qualisys are a very global business. We are industry leading
> within precision *motion capture* and 3D positioning tracking systems for engineering,
> biomechanics, animation, virtual reality, robotics and movement sciences. Our
> network around the world allows us to talk with customers in over 15 different

languages, allowing us to really understand our customers' needs and how to help them get the results they want.

Qualisys is certified according to ISO 9001:2015 and compliant with Medical Device Directive 93/42/EEC, which demonstrates our commitment to provide high quality products and services to our customers.

The Qualysis is an optical tracking method that uses infra-red reflecting markers on a performer that are recorded by multiple cameras to create data point clouds of an object in motion. The advantage of this method is that it uses a wavelength outside of visible light so as not to interfere with the visible light in the working environment. Systems that use visible light alone depend a great deal upon contrast of the figure against a white background and this is prone to errors of interpretation and a loss of accuracy. Other systems such as radio frequency positioning systems can be confronted with interference and static from local Internet, radio, and other signals. These systems seem to work best in an outside location isolated from buildings.

Setting up the camera cage

In the case of all optical systems, several cameras must be mounted on all sides of the performer to gather the movement data. For small stages, a bare minimum of four cameras can be used for all points of the compass but the

Figure 3.1 *Finding the center of the stage by projecting lines from opposite corners. The yellow light rings show the locations of the cameras. Courtesy of Mobile Motion MoCap.*

performer will be very limited in their movements, perhaps even needing to perform while standing in one position. In this example we will create a large truss composed of four major posts connected by four top cross braces to form a rectangular cage and an additional two braces at both far ends in order to mount extra cameras to cover the long dimension of the space. This space will need 41 cameras to capture the performance within the area known as "the volume." The first thing to do is to find the center of the space or zero point. This is easily done by projecting two lines from each opposing corner post to form an "X." The center of the X becomes the zero point upon which one places the "L" for calibration.

The "L"

The "L" is a collapsible mount with a set number of retroreflective balls attached to it. When the mount is expanded it forms an "L" shape with the extensions at a perfect 90-degree angle from each other. The bend of the "L" is placed at the center of the stage with the long arm extended along the long axis of the stage.

Reflection considerations

For the system to work properly it must only see the round target markers reflecting the infra-red radiation from each of the cameras. The system only expects to see the markers on the "L." On occasion the radiation from a camera may reflect off a glossy floor or perhaps a video monitor on the side lines used for assisting alignment and create a bogus marker signature. The physical ways to address such problems is to adjust monitors so they don't show reflections or in the case of the floor, one can use light carpet with a texture that will break up and absorb any reflection. In the software there are three

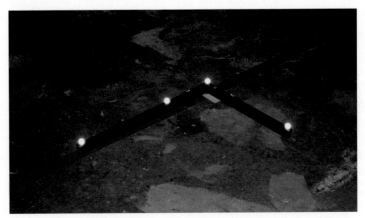

Figure 3.2 *The "L" bracket with four marker balls. The corner bracket is placed over the zero point with the longer arm along the long axis of the stage.*

remedies. The first option is to reduce the size of the marker area the camera is looking for to the size of the small retroreflective spheres. In this way the system will ignore any larger stray reflections off a floor. The second remedy is to create a garbage mask around the reflection to "hide" it from the system so that it is not seen by the offending camera. It is better to use several small masks instead of one large one to address reflections. One must remember that while the mask system is useful, it also will prevent any data from the performer being seen by the camera if the actor should move behind the masked area. This is often not a terrible problem as one has 38 extra cameras picking up the slack from other viewpoints. The third option is to put the flashing infra-red emitter on the camera causing the reflection to be slightly out of sync with the camera that is seeing the reflection. In this manner, each camera only sees the infra-red that it is emitting. This option is useful if the camera is seeing another camera.

Setting the cameras and the daisy chain

In this set-up there are 39 cameras that emit infra-red radiation from a circular ring around the lens and detect the reflection off the markers. There are an extra two video cameras that capture the space as a video image that can be used for superimposing the markers on top of the performer for analyzing, calibration and alignment. Each of the identical Miqus M1 cameras records at a frame rate of 250 frames per second (fps) at a resolution of 1216 × 800. The standard lens field of view is 50 by 40 degrees. There are two ethernet ports that carry both power and data so that the cameras can be easily "daisy chained" together for connection to the main computer/software interface. All the cameras should be adjusted for exposure so that they match. In the software, the threshold control helps make the image of the tracker balls all the same size. The exposure or video gain setting is adjusted so that the balls have no flicker. The intensity slider makes the markers brighter. Even if the "L" is not visible one should place temporary tracker balls in each camera view so that the threshold and exposure settings can be adjusted to match the other cameras. These temporary markers should be removed before the calibration process.

The basic idea is to position the cameras so that there is an overlap between their field of views. An example would be if the performer is standing in a "T" pose with arms outstretched then three Miqus cameras would be able to see either the full figure or at least a portion of the figure. Camera 1 might see the left arm, camera 2 would see the full figure, and the adjacent camera 3 would see the right arm. So, the positioning of the cameras must include the concept of overlap to cover as much three-dimensional area as possible. When daisy chaining the cameras, it is important to arrange them in groups as well, such as one side of the top long dimension will be one group and the other side would be the other. As the signals come in, each camera will be assigned a number by

Figure 3.3 *The Miqus camera with infra-red emitting light ring. The ring can also glow with visible light as an indicator of operational status. The camera amount allows for precise positioning. Courtesy of Mobile Motion MoCap.*

Figure 3.4 *The standard "T" pose used for marker calibration. Courtesy of Mobile Motion MoCap.*

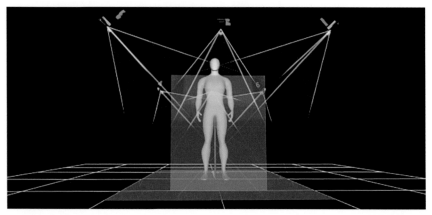

Figure 3.5 *The principle of overlapping fields of view when mounting cameras. Courtesy of Qualysis.*

the Qualysis software. It is helpful to write that number on a piece of tape and attach it to the physical camera to quickly spot cameras for adjustment. Each Miqus camera has a freely adjustable and lockable mount for positioning. In some cases, it may be beneficial to mount the camera so that its field of view is vertical instead of horizontal to facilitate the best capture space.

It is helpful when positioning cameras to place tape on the stage floor to form a grid. A common practice is to have one operator adjusting the camera while observing a large monitor in the distance that displays what that camera is seeing along with the tape borders on the floor. To assist the camera positioner (who may be far across the room) the assistant can hold a piece of white paper on top of the monitor image that aligns with the image of the tape border to make the camera adjustment easier when viewing the monitor's camera view from a distance.

The calibration wand

Once all the cameras are adjusted it will be time to calibrate the system in order to finalize and detect the volume that is being observed. For this, the "L" will be placed at the zero point and an operator will slowly walk about the performance space waving a "T" wand with two tracker balls in a slow figure of eight pattern all through the space. He or she will walk the length of the space and back again and perhaps taking extra time in corners. An assistant will activate the calibration recording and set the time for typically 180 seconds. The longer the time the more data will be collected and the more accurate the space will be. The point of the wand and the zero is not to identify where zero is but where all the cameras are in relation to each other. The assistant will call out the time so that the wand dancer can give the entire space equal coverage.

Figure 3.6 *The wand "dance" taking place for 180 to 360 seconds or more within the performance area to define the volume. The wand waver listens for the time countdown to ensure that equal time is given to all cameras to see the wand. Courtesy of Mobile Motion MoCap.*

Checking the volume

Once the calibration is completed the Qualysis system can determine the space covered and if there is any missing data after computing the calibration results. In a chart showing all the data captured for each camera a number will appear. The lower the number means the less data was captured, and this may require another wand "dance" to focus more on one or more cameras. There are also several views the operator can use to see how successful the volume creation is.

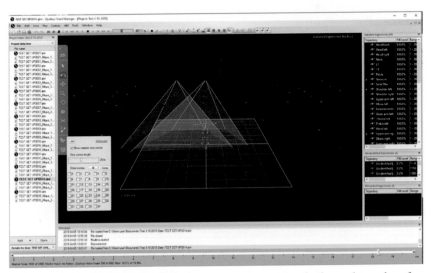

Figure 3.7 *By displaying the field of view cones we can more clearly see the overlap of two cameras. Courtesy of Qualysis.*

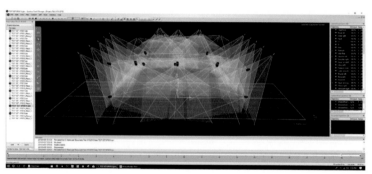

Figure 3.8 *By turning on all the cameras and displaying each cone we can get a confusing but accurate overall view. Courtesy of Qualysis.*

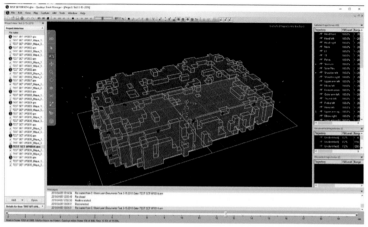

Figure 3.9 *This "Lego stack" view lets the operator see more clearly the bubble of area within the stack where the actor can have his or her performance captured. Courtesy of Qualysis.*

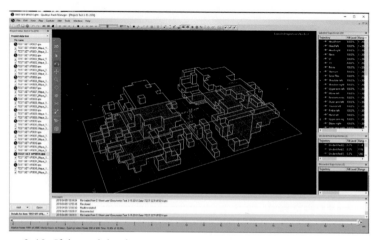

Figure 3.10 *If the stack has large gaps it means we have patches of missed data and the wand dance should be done again. Courtesy of Qualysis.*

Preparing the performer

The typical motion-capture suit is designed to be tight fitting, with little to no movement of the fabric as this would create inaccurate data. The marker balls are affixed to the suit with easily adjusted and removable Velcro attachments. There are a variety of schemes for the placement of the markers and this is just one example to determine where the joints of the figure are. When each marker is seen by the system it must be labeled to indicate what it represents such as "left elbow," "solar plexus," "right knee," etc.

One must remember that the computer is just an extremely fast adding machine that is very dumb. It must be told everything, and therefore each marker has a specific label so that it can be matched on top of a computer graphic character's rigged joints.

Assume the position

Once the markers are affixed and stable it is time for the performer to stand in the center of the stage and assume two positions to calibrate their markers. The first position is an "A" pose where the subject stands with arms outstretched to forms the sides of the "A." After a few seconds of recording the actor a "T" pose is struck with hands with palms downward to the floor. After a few seconds of the second pose the arms only are moved and then after a few seconds the legs are moved, and the recording is stopped. These static poses when converted to marker dots on the screen will help identify the different joints so that they can be labeled. Once this is done the computer will now know what

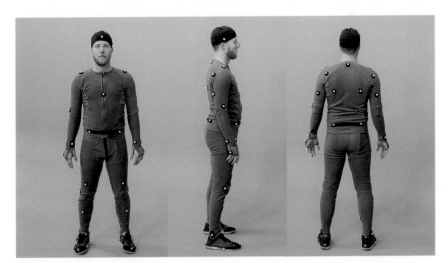

Figure 3.11 *A general marker placement on the suit. At long last the actor can finally transcend their physicality and play any character they wish or turn back the ravages of time. Courtesy of Mobile Motion MoCap.*

the marker dots represent and then can assign their position data to matching joints in the synthetic character.

Performance and patching

When everything has been calibrated the performance is captured and recorded. Even with 38 cameras there will be moments within the 250 fps recording where some markers will not be seen by either occlusion of limbs obscuring the markers or by being outside of the volume. Qualysis uses pattern recognition to sense directions of movements of the markers and deduces through assumption where a missing marker would be (even if it is not seen) and plugs in or patches a synthetic marker so that an arm, let's say, stays intact throughout its travel rather than just popping off and back on.

Inertial body capture systems

Another approach to motion capture is to use a suit implanted with many special sensors to record data instead of the camera approach. The Nansense system for example can use up to five sensors that can capture 9 degrees of freedom or directions of movement with absolute orientation. The sensors measure at 2000 degrees/sec using a tri-axial gyroscope, magnetometer, and 16G accelerometer to compute each sensor's position in space and orientation to the other sensors without the need for observation cameras. All the sensors are connected to a central processing unit that has a built-in data logger along with being able to output via hardwire or Wi-Fi to another computer for streaming data into a character for real time performance. These systems are very powerful and can also provide the capability of using sensor gloves to capture intricate finger movement without the inherent problems of occlusion that would come from an optical method.

The advantage of the Nansense system is the flexibility of the capture environment as no scaffold to support cameras needs to be constructed. An inertial sensor suit can work in small studios or even outdoors in a level area. The wireless signal has a range of 150 feet (46 meters) indoors and about 300 feet (92 meters) outdoors from the router. The main limitation is that the capture area must be free from magnetic and radio interference. Large metal objects can confuse the sensors, and offices with heavy Wi-Fi traffic can also create problems. I have found it helpful to demo the system in a variety of potential locations such as within a school to find an area that is free from interference issues. One must also keep in mind that any props the MoCap performer uses should be made of wood or plastic instead of metal to insure against interference.

Figure 3.12 *The Synertial inertial MoCap suit with capture gloves. Courtesy of Mobile Motion MoCap.*

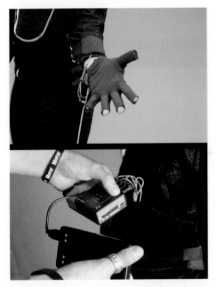

Figure 3.13 *Closer view of the Synertial glove and below the Synertial central processor, battery, and transmitter. Courtesy of Mobile Motion MoCap.*

Facial motion capture (back to optical)

Both the Faceware and the Dynamixyz systems use head gear that enables the system to light the face of the performer and a video camera to capture footage of their facial expressions that can be mapped to several blend shapes on a synthetic character's face. Blend shapes are very similar to traditional replacement animation where a series of unique mouth shapes could be attached to a stop-motion puppet to animate dialog. In the case of blend shapes a series of full-face expressions modeled in polygons, let's say a smile and a frown, can be goal points where the meshes of both face expressions can be morphed over time to smoothly transition from a smile to a frown with far more fidelity than could be achieved with traditional replacement methods.

Facial recognition has improved to the point that the systems are able to discern the edges of lips, eyes, and eyebrows on the face. Some productions may find it useful to use drawn markers on the face from time to time to record subtle movements of amorphous areas like cheeks or necks. While acceptable live-streaming results from facial motion capture can be obtained, some high-end productions require the use of artists to fine tune the positioning of meshes frame-by-frame to insure the faithful reproduction of an actor's performance and dialog. This is done by viewing a superimposition of the live actor's face atop the CG character and manipulating the lips mesh to align perfectly (if anatomy allows) with the edges of the live actor's lips. I'm confident that much of this type of fine tuning was needed for the spectacular Planet of the Apes films.

The blend shape method incorporated into Dynamixyz software has two sections. The first section is the grabber that captures the face motion and the second is the performer tool. This tool selects several facial profiles or expressions such as a smile, frown, sneer, etc. and connects the recognized points to the computer character model in Maya® software that has several sliders that warp the underlying mesh to drag the mouth into a smile or a frown key frame position. The blend shape mask controls are memorized for each facial profile. As the motion capture changes from frame to frame, the slider controls animate to move the mesh into the next appropriate face shape, softly blending the warp effect from one shape to another in real time.

Motion builder and the pipeline

Motion Builder is a 3D character animation software produced by Autodesk. At the time of writing, this is the go-to tool for supporting motion-capture devices. Basically, it takes the positional data from Qualysis, Nansense, and others and attaches those tracked motion points to a virtual skeleton allowing it to follow the live-action motion. This process of attaching the cloud of motion-capture "points" in space to specific areas of a synthetic skeleton is called retargeting or solving. The software also in turn allows that skeleton to manipulate the mesh and textures of the computer graphic model to allow the virtual character to perform. This tool like many others in the digital age may be in a transitional phase as motion-capture companies add their own retargeting tools to their products such as Qualysis. For now, Motion Builder

Figure 3.14 *The Dynamixyz face gear. The image below shows the traditional replacement animation of mouth positions that was the predecessor of the ultra-fluid blend shape methods used in computer graphics. Above image courtesy of Mobile Motion MoCap.*

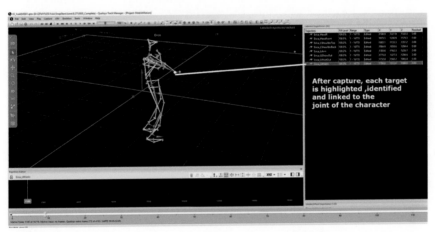

Figure 3.15 *The Qualysis retargeting solution. Courtesy of Qualysis.*

is an indispensable tool in our virtual pipeline. As an example for live streaming, we start with Qualysis whose data is sent to Motion Builder to solve and then a plug-in for Motion Builder called Live Link allows the mocap-controlled character to be inserted into the Unreal® Game Engine and in turn to compositing software in order to create an all-encompassing virtual studio combining game engine sets, live action, and virtual characters moving all together in real time.

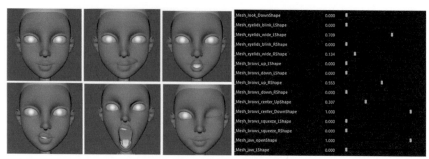

Figure 3.16 *To create blend shapes copies are made of a neutral face shown in the upper left and then distorted in a variety of expressions. Unlike standard replacement animation where faces are replaced as a whole, the computer allows the final face to be a combination of blend shape expressions that are blended by degree depending on the facial capture target positions. The sliders on the right show how different polygon mesh groups (digital muscles) are positioned by the sliders. When a facial mocap performance is captured one can see all the sliders vary their positions in real-time as the real actor performs. Courtesy of Mobile Motion MoCap.*

Now that we've given a brief survey of procedures to capture the performance of our live actors the next step is to capture the performance of our camera operator as the scenes are shot. The next chapter is an examination of techniques used to set up and track camera movement.

Chapter 4
Camera tracking

Chapter 1 discussed the transition from hand-animated repeat tracking to computer-controlled repeat moves using motion control and then to image-analysis tracking to move a virtual camera to match the live-action camera. In all these cases there was time needed in post to not only match moves but to put images together in compositing. Today we have real-time tracking where the live-action camera is tightly locked to its virtual counterpart within the Unreal® Game Engine.

This groundbreaking development gives us the promise of making virtual movies in the same time frame as traditional movies. In the past, compositing of elements always involved production and post. Green-screen live action was shot as an element and in post a virtual background was painstakingly match moved and lit to match the live action along with final compositing involving weeks of work. For synthetic characters a great deal of time was needed to create the computer graphic model and rig it for movement to be either animated or manipulated with motion capture. This was once again executed entirely in post along with compositing. "Real time" camera tracking and motion capture allows us to do all these operations simultaneously. When one looks through the camera of a virtual studio as it points at a performer in front of a green screen, one sees the entire composite at once. The live actor appears in the virtual background and performs alongside a synthetic character manipulated by a motion-capture artist. The camera is free to roam at will. The result is the same as if you were shooting a live actor in a real set alongside a performer in a rubber creature suit performing a scene together live as the camera dollies, pans, tilts, or zooms. We can now shoot virtual shots and performers as if they existed in real space. The challenge for the actors is to perform across from the invisible character and set within the green void. For the director and cinematographer everything is seen all at once on the monitor displaying the final product. The first step in achieving this miracle is the camera itself.

As the real camera moves so does its virtual twin much like motion capture. With motion capture the data points collected must be referenced to joints on our character model. With camera tracking data we must inform the computer system what the data represent as a spatial location. The following procedure describes this process as we set up our virtual stage with a camera tracking system.

The Halide FX system

The Halide FX system is the next generation of the Prevision system created by Eliot Mack the founder of Lightcraft Technology (https://hal idefx.com). The Prevision system was part of Universal Studios Virtual Stage One and was utilized on many high-end projects such as *Alice in Wonderland* (2010), *Man of Steel* (2013), *The Last Stand* (2013), "Pan Am" (2011–2012), and "The Last Man on Earth" (2015–2018) among others. The basic concept is the use of a tracking camera mounted on top of a live-action camera. The tracking camera has a lens pointed upward toward several targets on the ceiling to measure and report where the live-action camera is in space. This data is instantly transmitted to a virtual camera in a computer-graphic environment that becomes a virtual clone of the live-action camera. The two cameras will move together in synchronization. The live-action performers are positioned in front of a green screen and are composited in real time into the computer graphic environment. The director can see the composite instantly complete with matched camera moves. For high-end feature films, it becomes a previz tool that renders in real-time, high-definition resolution. The raw 4K recording of the live action is then later composited with 4K rendered computer-graphic environments in post. In the case of television production, the high-definition output generated on stage can be cut directly into the show.

Halide FX is a refinement of the system based on the numerous industry projects mentioned above. It is a less expensive, streamlined system with a friendly user interface for rapid adoption of virtual set technology.

The constellation of targets

The targets that are usually placed on the ceiling are composed of three graphics of different sizes that the computer will recognize as an individual number. The three sizes are to facilitate varying distances of the tracking camera to the targets. A low to the ground camera will track using the larger symbols. A camera booming up to the ceiling will make use of the mid-size and smallest symbols to continue the track. At different distances the demarcation between the black and white parts of the target will always be clear on at least one section of the targets for a smooth track. Depending on the size of the stage used the overall size of the three-symbol target will be adjusted. Large stages will have large targets and smaller stages will make do with smaller targets. The targets are easily affixed to a pipe grid on the ceiling, making sure that the grid is stable and not subject to movement. While the ceiling is the most effective area to place the targets, they can also be placed along a wall or the floor if needed. An example of this would be an extreme tilt up where the tracking camera looking up at the ceiling will soon be tilted away from its view of the targets and lose the track. If the targets are along the wall and the tracking camera positioned to look to the side, then the tracking camera will always have them in view for the full extreme tilt.

Figure 4.1 *A Halide tracking target with three different-sized symbols that represent numbers to the computer. The virtual stage set-up shows the placement of the targets atop the ceiling. If one or more of the targets are occluded during a move the remaining physical targets will maintain an accurate track. Courtesy of Mobile Motion MoCap, target image courtesy of Lightcraft.*

Figure 4.2 *Live-action camera with the tracker camera mounted on top. The umbilical cord sends tracking data and video to the computer and receives the video signal of the composite so that it can be displayed on the taking camera's monitor.*

The closer view of the Halide tracking camera shows the sensor position marked on top and a dimple marker on the side to locate the sensor for measurements.

Defining the space

In the past, a complex process of using surveying tools was utilized to obtain an accurate measurement of the stage space. The Halide system uses the tracking camera itself to perform this duty in a far more expedient manner. First the tracking camera is detached from the live-action camera. With the tracking camera lens pointed upward the technician walks about the space so that the computer can see and recognize the targets. This process only takes a minute or two and is finished when the image of the targets on the tracking camera monitor all turn from yellow to green. At this point the computer recognizes all the targets in space but has no idea of the size of the targets or if they are positioned inside a warehouse or a dollhouse, or how high the targets are from the floor and the flatness of the floor. To obtain a distance relationship the tracking camera is placed in a convenient place on the stage floor that will be used as ground zero or the universal reference for the space in both the real world and the computer graphic virtual world. This can be the same center point as described in the mocap chapter (Chapter 3). A metric measuring tape is placed alongside the zero point and stretched about 3 meters along one axis of the floor. The track camera is placed at the zero point using an arbitrary spot on the camera body such as a screw, rail, or edge.

This camera position is recognized by the system and recorded and then the track camera is moved a few meters further down the line to capture the view of this second location. The camera is then moved to the side by a similar distance to record a third position.

Using the parallax displacement of these three points, the computer can now figure out how high the floor is from the targets and the flatness of the floor.

Measuring the camera sensor offsets

This process can be a bit trickier as any number of cameras can be used for the live-action portion and will vary by design. The goal is to get as close as possible to measure the relative locations of both the live-action sensor and the tracking-camera sensor so that the computer thinks of them as one and the same camera. The position data that is sent to the virtual computer graphic

Figure 4.3 *Measuring the side-to-side distance relationship from the center of both lenses in centimeters. In this case 4.3 cm.*

Figure 4.4 *In some cases one must be careful with certain camera designs. Note that the sensor marking on the live-action camera (the line and circle focus icon just below the 15 cm label) is correct for measuring distance for focus by attaching a tape measure to the focus post below but is incorrect for the up/down orientation. The sensor is obviously directly behind the lens and not at the focus icon position. We measure from the center of the lens and sensor as indicated by the tracking camera's dimple at the top to the center of the live-action camera lens at the bottom. This distance is 15 cm.*

camera will be accurate only if it will account for the offset of the tracking-camera and live-camera sensors.

You now must measure the height difference between sensors.

The final measured offset is the forward offset (as seen in Figure 4.5) measuring the distance each sensor is apart from each other front to back. This would be the measurement from the line and circle icon to the edge of the tape which projects down the position of the tracking camera's sensor above.

Once the camera offsets are input, a final physical measurement is taken from the center of the lens at level camera to the floor to verify that the actual height of the camera is within 1 cm of what the tracking camera states the height is. This is an important confirmation before moving on to the tilt, pan, and roll adjustments. These fine-tune adjustments are made by tilting up so that the live camera sees the targets while an overlay of the output positions is seen on top of the targets. If these positions do not fit in the center of the targets then slight adjustments of the offsets need to be made in order to make the tracking points lie on top of the physical targets viewed on the ceiling as shown in Figure 4.6.

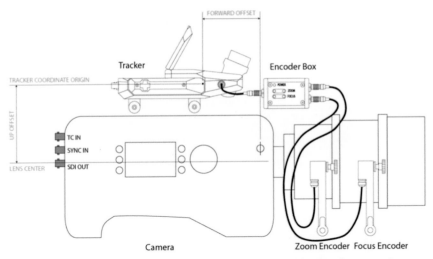

Figure 4.5 *The Halide diagram of camera measurements. Note that the camera lens has encoders to electronically measure the focus and zoom positions. Halide FX diagram, courtesy of Lightcraft.*

Figure 4.6 *The tracking points are displayed atop the video image of the targets themselves for fine adjustments. The box insert displays the offset orientation between the tracker camera and the live-action camera. In this case fine tuning is needed to fit the tracking points on top of the targets. Courtesy of Lightcraft.*

Zoom and focus data

Encoders affixed to the camera lens controls of zoom and focus (as shown in Figure 4.5) send signals to the system along with the tracking-camera data to lock in perfect synchronization between the real and virtual cameras. Once established, a synthetic green "box" is created within the software that fits atop the virtual matching location of the live green-screen area. The box will

Synthetic Green Screen "box" overlaid on real screen to create a garbage matte.

Figure 4.7 *The synthetic green backing used as a garbage matte in the Halide system. Courtesy of Lightcraft.*

mask out the area outside of the green screen to allow the composite of the background to continue beyond the live-action green-screen area. Chroma key tools within the Halide system will achieve the task of compositing the live performers into the virtual location. For optimal performance Lightcraft suggests compositing the performers standing on a real floor to capture true to life contact shadows and interaction. The astounding recreation of the Pan Am terminal made use of minimal walkways laid atop the green-screen floor to enhance the realism of the composite.

The Mo-Sys system

Another tracking system that hails from Britain also has an impressive list of projects under the company's belt such as *Life of Pi* (2012) and *Gravity* (2013). From their site:

> Using retro-reflective stickers that are stuck to the ceiling, an upwards-looking sensor known as StarTracker is mounted onto a headset or a camera, calculating its position using the stickers as a reference. This space can be expanded infinitely allowing for a wide variety of applications. This cost effective method enables wall-to-wall, multi-level tracking across the largest of environments; and it is totally resilient to changes in light even when objects are partially obstructing the StarTracker sensor.
>
> (https://www.mo-sys.com)

One advantage the StarTracker system has over Halide is the use of retrore-flective targets that are illuminated by the tracking camera itself with infra-red radiation that is invisible to the eye and live-action camera instead of patterned targets that need to be lit by an additional light source emitting light waves within the visual and photographic spectrum as in the Halide system. While a minor issue one might imagine lighting challenges on rare occasions during

Figure 4.8 *The constellation of retroreflective targets. In this case the targets are attached to a flexible tarp. One must be sure that the tarp is taught and not near any air ducts or fans that could make the tarp flex and move in a draft. You don't want "moving" targets in a camera-tracking system. Courtesy of Mobile Motion MoCap.*

Figure 4.9 *The StarTracker camera atop the live-action camera. The monitor viewfinder displays the constellation above. Courtesy of Mo-Sys Engineering Ltd.*

Mo-Sys StarTracker workflow diagram

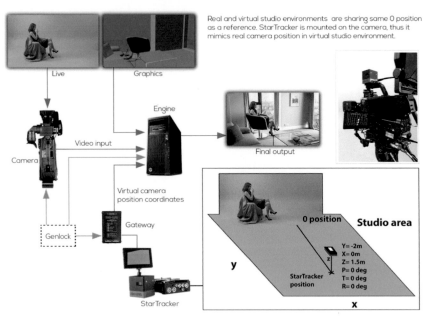

Figure 4.10 *The Mo-Sys work flow. Courtesy of Mo-Sys Engineering Ltd.*

production when using customary lighting instruments to light the targets. The great advantage of the tried and true Halide method is that it is a turnkey system with all parts of the process contained in one system. Independent trackers like Mo-Sys, while excellent, can be challenged by the ever–changing updates in the wide number of compositing systems that it can be connected to. It is a constant challenge for specialized tools and software to keep up with changes in the software they interact with. When planning a production, it is good practice to verify that plug-ins and combinations of software "play well with each other" as an unexpected upgrade in one that has not been addressed by another can create issues.

With this system we use random retroreflective targets of a variety of sizes depending upon the height of the ceiling. The StarTracker camera like the Qualysis system emits infra-red radiation that reflects off the targets and images their location on the camera sensor. The calibration method is like the Halide method where the StarTracker camera is placed on the floor looking up at the constellation. One measures from the camera on the floor to the ceiling and inputs that measurement. When prompted by the software the camera is moved a specific distance until a preliminary map is made. At this point the camera can be picked up and carried by the technician to find and locate all the other targets merely by moving about slowly around the stage as the target stars get registered in the system.

Referencing the map

Once the system sees the constellation it only does so within its own world and has no idea where the real world is so we must drop three points into the system. The first point is the Origin, which is where the camera is positioned. The second point is the Y axis, which is where the talent stands in front of the camera lens. The third and most important point is 90 degrees to the right (as seen from behind the camera), which is the X axis. The greater the distance from 0 to X, the greater the accuracy of the StarTracker mapping. 0–X is roughly ½ of the studio height or ⅓ of the width.

At this point the tracker camera is attached to the production camera's body and fine-tuning adjustments are made like the illustrations of the target alignment method of Halide to lock in the tracking so that the subject remains fixed in relation to the environment to eliminate sliding or misregistration of the subject as the production camera moves.

A recent innovation by the company is the ability for the system to ascertain the sensor offsets without inputting manual measurements. The common denominator between the systems is to acquire accurate measurements by whatever means to let the tracking systems know both the size of the environment and the offsets between the sensors.

The StarTracker system also adds encoders to the lens to record zoom and focus positions along with the positional data.

Mapping the live-action lens

Both the Halide and the StarTracker system will need the live-action lens mapped so that a data file can be created that contains its unique lens attributes. This file can then be plugged into graphic systems so that even the unique lens distortions of the live-action lens can be added to the tracking data to create a perfect virtual twin of the live camera within the synthetic environment.

Why we map lenses

Before lenses, pinhole cameras were used to collect single light rays reflected off the subject to form a sharp but extremely dim image onto the film. Lenses enabled us to collect many more rays of light reflected off the subject and focus them onto the film. Since the light rays go through many pieces of convex and concave glass lenses, there are inevitable distortions that occur that can also affect each of the three wavelengths (i.e. red, green, and blue light rays) individually. These distortions have many names such as chromatic (color) aberrations, pinhole distortion, and barrel distortion to name a few. As an

Figure 4.11 *The problem of lens distortion when compositing.*

example of how this affects a composite, Figure 4.11 composites a perfect undistorted rectangular wanted poster onto a wooden building. As the camera is panned note how the boards distort unevenly and began to pull away from the poster destroying the illusion. The track may be perfect as shown by the lower left-hand corner of the poster but as the poster does not distort in the same way it ceases to fit against the board as in the upper frame. Capturing the lens characteristics allow the graphic software to either add the same distortion to the virtual camera lens or be able to undistort the real-world image to fit into a virtual perfect lens world. The lens file also prevents the sliding of the live-action performers atop of a synthetic floor and other anomalies.

More on mapping

David Stump, ASC, in his excellent book, *Digital Cinematography: Fundamentals, Tools, Techniques, and Workflows* (Focal Press, 2014), points out the importance of capturing lens data:

> Lens mapping is crucial to the success of doing visual effects work. Precise measure-
> ment of lens characteristics can make the difference between expensive visual effects

work and economical visual effects work, usually accomplished by meticulously shooting grid charts through a wide variety of focus and zoom positions in order to reverse engineer the design geometry of lenses. The optics that make lenses rectilinear must be fully measured and understood in order to integrate computer generated images into live action cinematography.

Zoom lenses complicate the issues of lens geometry because they move many elements in relation to each other in order to change focal length, making it extremely hard to understand what is happening to the image in terms of optical geometry correction.

Anamorphic lenses further complicate the issues of lens geometry because they almost always have an optical path with two different ray-trac cross nodal points! The anamorphic (squeeze) element only functions in the horizontal axis of the lens and has its own nodal point, different than the vertical axis, vastly complicating the calculation of lens distortion and geometry, and making the work of integrating CGI an order of magnitude more difficult, especially in moving shots.

As one might imagine, this lens mapping or calibration requires a dedicated professional or service to be done properly and that is why tracking firms such as Halide and Mo-Sys offer a list of pre-mapped lenses as well as lens-mapping services for clients.

The calibration procedure

In order to map a lens a high-resolution sensor is used to record an image of special targets through the lens being mapped. If it is a zoom lens, data is obtained from a full range of focus and focal length settings as shown for example in the chart below for a 28–105 mm Canon zoom lens.

Focus settings	3 feet	5 feet	10 feet	20 feet	infinity	
Zoom settings						
28 mm	3 feet	5 feet	10 feet	20 feet	infinity	
35 mm	3 feet	5 feet	10 feet	20 feet	infinity	
50 mm	3 feet	5 feet	10 feet	20 feet	infinity	
70 mm	3 feet	5 feet	10 feet	20 feet	infinity	
105 mm	3 feet	5 feet	10 feet	20 feet	infinity	

The Focal length is held at 28 mm while the focus is set to 3 feet to take a picture of the chart or targets. After that exposure the focus only is changed to 5 feet and another picture is taken and so on to the infinity setting. After that exposure the zoom is changed to 35 mm and the same focus run is made again to obtain a matrix of the entire focus range against the full range of focal lengths.

The images are then taken into software for analysis to derive a lens map unique to that lens. This data is then used in real-time tracking and compositing systems to create a flawless composite between the real and the unreal.

The next step

While Halide has its own compositing tool that comes with the system, Mo-Sys gives the option of supplying tracking and lens data to independent graphic software such as the Zero Density Reality™ system. Mo-Sys also has an Unreal® plug-in that allows the data to control virtual cameras in Unreal® directly along with a chroma keyer to execute composites of live action within the sets in real time. All the tracking data and raw image elements can be recorded separately and put together later in post if higher resolution is needed. What follows in an examination of the Reality™ system, which is a unique compositing tool that is node-based with menu drop-downs, that accepts nearly every tracking tool on the market to combine live action into virtual environments.

Chapter 5

Under the hood of the Reality Engine™ compositing system

Reality Engine™

The Reality Engine™ compositing system created by Zero Density is a very deep, complex, and fabulous software that enables any number of real-time solutions for virtual filmmaking. This is where all the parts come together to create the final product.

In this examination I will break down the basic pipeline of the composite with cyclorama (or cyc) template in this software in order to create a 3D composite of live actors shot against a green screen into an Unreal® environment. There are several other ready-made pipeline templates in the system for rapid set-up of a variety of production situations such as augmented reality.

This node-based software connects a collection of unique tools together represented by nodes that have a single duty such as camera tracking. Each node will have a specific function and include a set of tools. Each node will be imbedded in a larger network of other nodes to enable the virtual studio. As was mentioned in Chapter 1, the idea of nodes was introduced early on with systems such as Cineon and continue to serve us well with current compositing tools such as Nuke™. As the layout can be complex, I will begin by breaking down the pipeline into large groups of nodes and their overall function and then choose smaller groups for a more detailed examination of the pipeline sections.

Reality Engine™ set pipeline

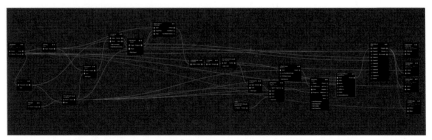

Figure 5.1 *The Reality Engine™ pipeline for live key with cyclorama. It's so simple a 5-year-old child could put it together. Does anyone know where I can find a 5-year-old child?*

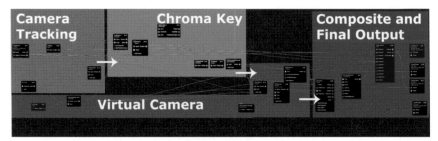

Figure 5.2 *This is a breakdown of the general functions of the major groups of nodes.*

The AJA video Input/Output (I/O) Device Node

The live-action portion of the tree starts with the AJA Device Node that can be seen in the upper left corner of Figure 5.1. Please note that the letters don't stand for the function of the device. They are merely the first letters of the names of special people known to the engineer and founder of AJA, John Abt. This node represents a piece of hardware inside the computer that distributes SDI video input and output signals. When you single-click on any node you will open the controls available for the node as seen in Figure 5.3. In this case Channel one is an input from the digital live-action camera whose output is 1080 p (progressive) at a frame rate of 29.97. A wide assortment of resolutions and frame rates can be handled by the AJA.

AJA input, Mo-Sys track mod, Cam 1 and ZD delay section

The AJA device is connected to the Zero Density (ZD) AJA input that obtains all the details of the selected channel (video channel one) and has pins for distributing the video and timecode information down the line. The timecode

Figure 5.3 *The AJA device and its controls.*

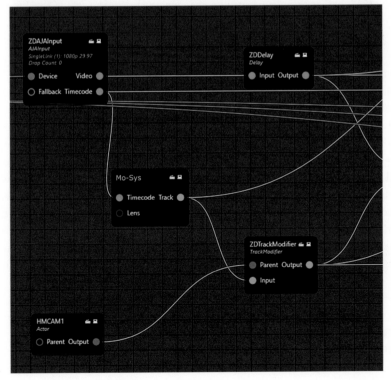

Figure 5.4 *Image prep stage one.*

information is fed into the Tracking Node (in this case Mo–Sys) to create the universal tracking information that allows the movement of the live-action camera to control the movement of the virtual twin camera inside Unreal®. Note that the Tracking Node has a lens input that is normally connected to a custom lens node that has mapped the distortions of the actual lens used on the camera. In this case all the lens information has been added within this Tracking Node. The track output sends the location data of where the live-action camera is in 3D space derived from the camera looking up at the retroreflective targets on the ceiling. The track output is going to a ZD Track Modifier Node that is essentially like a distributor so the same signal can be sent to multiple locations. At first glance this may seem like a superfluous node as the Tracking Node could also send multiple strings of data. The advantage of the modifier is that it can modify the track information before distribution. As a case in point, the Reality™ stage utilized a blue screen in the original stage set-up on the West side of the stage. Later it was decided green would be better and that screen was placed on the East side of the stage. This position is 180 degrees off from the original screen position. To save the effort of modifying all the previous set-ups and sets, you merely go into the Modifier and rotate the track info 180 degrees to quickly re-orient the space.

The HMCam1 is the virtual camera at its original position inside the Unreal® set. When it is connected as the parent it will be slaved to the movement of the live camera.

The ZD Delay Node delays anything connected to it. In this example, the ZD Delay Node is used to add latency to the video signal processing. To explain the need for this we must remember that while the speed of light in a vacuum is 186,000 miles per second. Electricity moves through copper wire at about 1/100th of that speed. In fact, it is so slow that the actual length of the wire can affect the synchronization of signals. One might imagine having red, green, and blue signals traveling through different lengths of wire. A 1-foot red wire would deliver its data much faster than 10-foot-long green and blue wires creating potential color distortion. In the case of the Delay Node we have so much tracking information traveling through any number of systems and wires that it is helpful to delay the video by a frame or two so that when you move the live-action camera the Unreal® background moves in sync with it (instead of "catching up").

Undistort and cyclorama section
Undistort

From the Delay Node we further modify the video signal by adding an Undistort Node. One might ask what you are undistorting as the video image

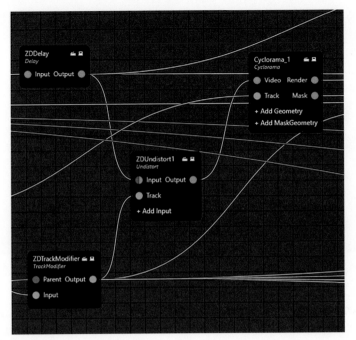

Figure 5.5 *Undistort and cyclorama.*

looks great. In fact, the video image has the subtle distortions brought about by shooting through a glass lens. Barrel distortion will slightly curve the image at the edges of the frame, pin cushion does the opposite by pinching in. Every lens is different, and the distortions will change throughout the zoom range as well. The Reality™ system mathematically maps these distortions to correct them. Why? Because the lens on the virtual camera has no distortions and always has straight lines and a perfect image. The Undistort Node makes the real lens as perfect as the virtual lens so that the cyclorama will function. The synthetic cyclorama is the key to the brilliant 3D compositing system devised by Zero Density.

Cyclorama

Within the Cyclorama Node we create a virtual green screen in the dimensions and shape of the actual screen. The dimensions of the real screen and its position in relation to the zero point on the stage floor are measured and used to create a polygon mesh that is slightly smaller and placed in the same virtual space within the Unreal® environment. Figure 5.5 shows the early stages of the cyclorama creation before final positioning and lengthening of the floor. The default cyc has three walls and a floor with coves for corners. In this case, because we only have a back wall and a floor, we are making a cyc to match.

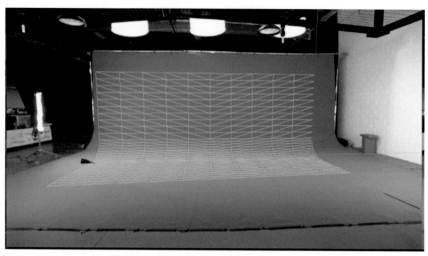

Figure 5.6 *Creating a synthetic matching cyclorama. Courtesy of Mobile Motion MoCap.*

Clean plate concept

Once the cyclorama polygon mesh is created, a still image is captured of the empty green stage from the live-action camera and used as a texture map on top of the virtual cyclorama. In this way we introduce a bit of the "real" green screen with shadows, wrinkles, stains, and all, into its virtual duplicate. Why? This creates a marvelous reference for the Reality Keyer™ so it can compare what is the screen by itself against the same screen with the live performer. This frame-by-frame comparison for every position allows

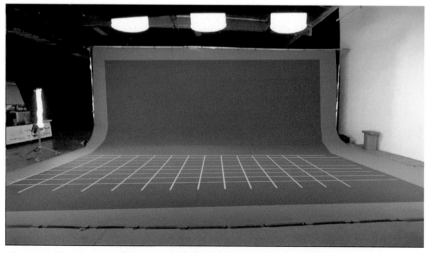

Figure 5.7 *Clean plate position. The clean plate area has been darkened for purposes of illustration along with the partial reveal of the mesh that the clean plate image is texture-mapped upon. Courtesy of Mobile Motion MoCap.*

the Reality Keyer™ to reproduce excellent shadows, transparent objects, and ultra-fine detail.

Mask

This same cyclorama is also used to create a garbage mask with soft edges that eliminates all the "garbage" beyond the green screen such as lights, C stands, personnel, etc. surrounding the live-action set. The beauty of this is that our live-action camera can pan 360 degrees to view the entire Unreal® set while our garbage mask continues to hide the unwanted real-world elements. To prevent gaps, the cyclorama is always created slightly within the area of the actual green screen to allow the edge to be feathered (softened) if needed.

Re-distort

The re-distort mode adds the physical lens distortion to the perfect computer graphic cyclorama so that it blends perfectly with the real green screen.

Reality Keyer™

The Reality Keyer™ Node is the main control for the compositing outcome of the result. The Reality Keyer™ has multiple controls that cross over with other controls and act much like a seesaw where one adjustment calls for a counter adjustment and so on. As a result, each composite situation will be unique and different depending on the details of the subject and the lighting.

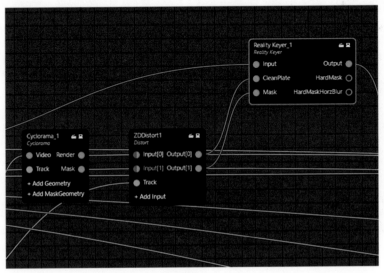

Figure 5.8 *Re-distorting the perfect cyclorama.*

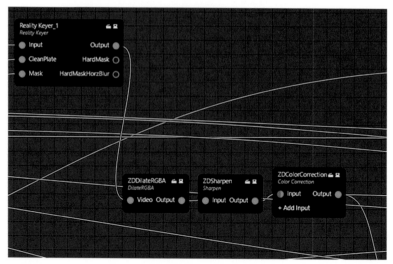

Figure 5.9 *Chroma keyer and fine-tuning nodes.*

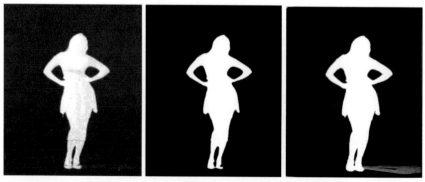

Figure 5.10 *The mask on the left is the raw input before final adjustments that include the addition of the clean plate. The middle mask is the shrunken core mask that prevents transparency in the center of the subject while allowing for another softer mask to resolve fine detail and shadows on the edges. The mask on the right shows the final adjusted mask combined with the core mask complete with shadow detail.*

The main philosophy of the matte controls is to adjust separate gammas for soft matte one and two. The word "gamma" can be thought of as contrast. "Soft matte" refers to the delicate matte or alpha channel that can resolve soft edges and shadows. Gamma one refers to the highlight end of the image while Gamma two addresses the darker shadow side. Both are adjusted together to obtain the cleanest matte (white on black) with soft variable density shadows. The clean plate comes into play as well to assist in creating the perfect matte. The perfect matte in this case has the most detailed edges and finely gradated shadow areas but would in most cases introduce holes or transparent spots in the middle of the subject. To address this, other controls come into play called the core matte. This does not resolve shadows but creates a hard edge matte of the figure that is bullet proof, meaning none of the background image has a chance of showing through. This "core" matte is in turn shrunk so that its edge that can be softened is well within the soft high-detail edge of the soft matte. When all are combined it yields a spectacular high-quality matte for compositing.

After the main Keyer Node the system follows up with a node for adjusting the shape of the matte. So, if you have everything perfect but see a dark line around a nose in profile you can use the Dilate Node to shrink the mask in one dimension to eliminate any dark lines around the subject. Following that you have a Sharpen Node that is self-explanatory for the foreground (FG) element and lastly a Color Correction Node for blending the color of the FG with the background (BG).

The projection cube section

After the Reality Keyer™ obtains the final perfect composite its output goes to another Undistort Node to make the image perfect again for placement by the Projection Node. One can think of this as making a perfect paper doll cut out of the live action that sits inside the 3D Unreal® set. The live action becomes

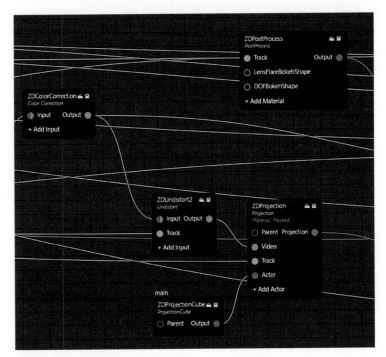

Figure 5.11 *The projection cube connection.*

not only a high-quality composite but also an element for creating transparency, refraction, and reflection effects that appear within the Unreal® set. At the bottom of Figure 5.9 is the all-important ZD Projection Cube Node. When disconnected from the actor pin, an image of a colorful cube will appear in the set. Its position within the set will determine what is in front of the live action and what is behind.

Figure 5.12 *The image above shows the Unreal® set before disconnecting and positioning the projection cube. Positioning the cube within the set below. Note that the screen and stand prop is in the middle of the cube meaning that live-action subjects positioned at the cube location will be behind the screen prop. Courtesy of Mobile Motion MoCap.*

Figure 5.13 *The Unreal® set before the cube insertion. Courtesy of Mobile Motion MoCap.*

Figure 5.14 *The projection cube is inserted within the set but behind the foreground pillar on the left. Courtesy of Mobile Motion MoCap.*

Figure 5.15 *When the cube is disconnected and the keyer activated the performer is composited within the three-dimensional space. Note how the soft reflection of his shirt highlights the pillar enhancing the realism of the composite. Courtesy of Mobile Motion MoCap.*

Figure 5.16 *Positioning the cube forward in front of the pillar. Courtesy of Mobile Motion MoCap.*

Figure 5.17 *This position of the cube allows the subject to be in front of the pillar. The high-quality image of the performer sits on top of the low-resolution copy (responsible for reflections of the performer on the set itself). 3D compositing allows the actor to perform within the 3D space and interact by casting shadows and reflections. Courtesy of Mobile Motion MoCap.*

Post process section

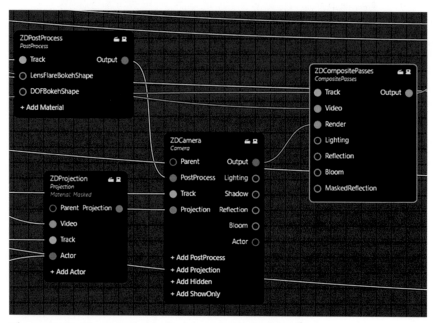

Figure 5.18 *The nodes for blending the real with the Unreal®.*

Post Process Node

The Post Process Node deals with the appearance of the Unreal® set by adjusting exposure, motion blur, and the like.

Camera Node

The controls of the virtual camera are essentially bookkeeping to insure an accurate match with the live-action camera such as sensor size, field of view, resolution, frame rate, etc.

Composite Passes Node

The Composite Passes Node combines the untouched (only keyed) live-action image with the image generated by the virtual camera (multiple passes) while having the tracking align both together perfectly.

The mixer engine and outputs section

The last leg of our trip is the Mixer Node that routes all the different signals such as the raw live-action camera footage, the composite, the alpha (mask)

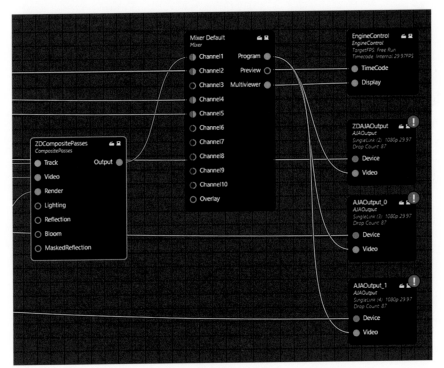

Figure 5.19 *The mixer and final outputs.*

channel, etc. to different Output Nodes to be recorded as separate elements should there be a need to fine tune in post. The Engine Node is responsible for keeping all these elements together and creating the multi-viewer that displays all the channels on one screen such as the raw green element, the composite, the mask, and other elements.

So that in a nutshell is the bare bones of the Reality Engine™ system. This is but one of several templates that are pre-connected to address the needs of several situations such as augmented reality where synthetic props are combined with live action. It is truly a remarkable system based on decades of the best tech developments of the past all rolled together to obtain a fantastic real-time compositing tool for the virtual backlot.

Chapter 6
Making a storyboard with Unreal® Engine

Preface to Chapter 6

Imagine you're a passenger on a plane where the pilot has just died, and you are asked to land the plane by getting instructions from the tower. Well, that is like what I will attempt to relate in these bare bones descriptions of how to navigate the Unreal® Engine. I will essentially relate how to launch the tool, load a set, create a camera, move it around, create some lights to light the set, and then use customary screen grab software to snatch the images to make a storyboard using Photoshop®. It will be very helpful to be familiar with Photoshop® as that is half the battle and will inform your progress if you should decide to navigate through Unreal®. This section is for readers who are primarily filmmakers or cinematographers who don't want to become Unreal® experts but want to know enough to convey ideas to an Unreal® artist. In truth you can also just use plain pencil and paper and draw your own storyboard and skip this section but I find it helpful to actually drive the system in a limited way so as to better communicate with and appreciate the technical artists who can really pilot this amazing software.

The Unreal® Engine

The key to this examination of the virtual studio is the Unreal® Engine developed by Epic Games. This astounding tool allows creators to create and animate virtual environments and characters for games and other media. The software interface is so incredibly complex and deep that it requires a separate study all of its own. For absolute beginners I would suggest *Unreal® Engine 4 Game Development in 24 Hours* by Aram Cookson, Ryan Dowling Soka, and Clinton Crumler (Sams Publishing, 2016). While the title is promising I assure you that it will be the longest 24 hours of your life. Just the fact that the book needs three distinguished authors shows you how deep this rabbit hole goes. While one can avail oneself of excellent software products such as Storyboard Pro, I have found that if one can use the actual location to previsualize while at the same time set camera locations and pre-light the set, the advantages are profound. In order to do this, I feel the aesthetically inclined filmmaker or director who is not tech savvy can surf Unreal® with a minimum of software learning-curve distraction. When one goes into actual production the team will most certainly include an Unreal® artist. This artist can also quickly adopt the Reality™ software to integrate the two programs together as Reality™ rides on top of Unreal® to create the virtual studio. It would be a huge plus to have a Reality™ artist as well as to provide excellent green-screen pulls and to program animation events within the scene. This means that if the equipment has enough processing power to record real-time high-resolution finished composites with sound it can be possible to come close to the speed of a traditional film or television shoot.

The Unreal® Marketplace

The Marketplace allows one to shop for virtual environments at an incredibly low price point and if used in a media other than games are royalty free according to the terms and conditions on the website under Section 4 (https://www.unrealengine.com/en-US/eula).

> However, no royalty is owed on the following forms of revenue:
>
> 4. Revenue from an Unrestricted Product, including for clarity, revenue from a Product which solely relies on the Licensed Technology for production of non-interactive linear media (e.g., broadcast or streamed video files, cartoons, or movies) and which is Distributed in a form that does not contain the Licensed Technology or, in order to deliver, rely on servers running the Licensed Technology.

I include this clause for information only and not to be construed as legal advice as I am not an attorney. Before embarking on a project, I whole heartedly recommend that an attorney be consulted to go over the terms and conditions to make sure that all parties are happy, and you comply with the rules and are not subject to copyright infringement.

Shopping in the Unreal® Marketplace

The catalog of environments and props is spectacular but can be confusing when looking over the technical specifications. As a guide I will highlight one set that works particularly well for the Zero Density Reality Engine™ system.

Here is a link for the Victorian Street created by Richard Vinci:

https://www.unrealengine.com/marketplace/en-US/slug/victorian-street

The price for this impressive set is AMAZING at only $20 and the rating of 35 is confidence building. The most important section here is the Supported Engine Versions, which in this case are 4.16–4.21. Always check to see that your Engine version matches the version the set was designed for.

If we explore further into the technical details, we see that all 20 elements (blueprints) are not locked together and much like a real movie set, walls and props can be moved without all the physical challenges of a real full-size set. Real backlot sets that can't be moved are often built with streets running from North to South so when the sun rises in the East and sets in the West, this guarantees that each side of the street will always be in pleasant ambient light for at least half the day. In the case of the virtual backlot you have complete control over lighting.

The texture size specification demonstrates the detail that is contained within the set. If your project's final movie resolution is 1920 × 1080 you will have

Figure 6.1 *Watching the video samples of the set demonstrates the impressive amount of work. Chimneys have animated smoke that cast shadows on the ground and flags wave in the wind (https://www.youtube.com/watch?v=guYsC_C8LUU&feature=youtu.be).*

Technical Details

Features:

- 20 Blueprints that make it easy to find, place, and modify assets
- Spline Blueprints that allow great flexibility in the placement and shape of roads, sidewalks, and rooftops
- 130+ meshes designed for a modular workflow
- Master materials and material instances that make it easy control the appearance of the meshes
- Vertex-paintable materials for creating dirt and water accumulation

Texture Sizes:

- 1 at 4096x4096
- 244 at 2048x2048
- 57 smaller than 2048x2048

Collision: Yes, automatically generated
Vertex Count: Mostly less than 2000, Max: 3919
LODs: Yes (List)
Number of Meshes: 149
Number of Materials and Material Instances: 131
Number of Textures: 302
Supported Development Platforms: Windows
Supported Target Build Platforms: Windows
Documentation: Yes

Figure 6.2 *Technical specifications listed in the marketplace for the Victorian set.*

no problem with loss of resolution or pixilation as you get close to portions of the set. It isn't clear what part of the set is in 4096 × 4096 resolution, but I suspect it may be a clock. With this high resolution you would be able to move in very close to highlight a few numbers on the clock with the utmost clarity. For a high-definition program, 244 of the textures used for the street, walls, sidewalk, etc. come in at 2048 × 2048, which is more than enough resolution.

The Collision specification of yes prevents models from vanishing into one another. This would be useful for the waving flags to keep the cloth whole as it moves. A vertex is the point where the lines of a polygon join. The phrase "Mostly less than 2000, Max 3919" is a good clue of what to look for in the vertex section when choosing other sets. LOD stands for level of detail. The number of materials (131), meshes (149), and textures (302) demonstrate the flexibility of the set as it has so many modifiable pieces.

Level of detail

The level of detail is a design term for video game sets where rendering speed is increased by using the maximum number of polygons when an object is close and reducing the polygon count as the object moves farther away in the distance. A barrel with many staves may have 100 polygons when seen up close but if moved off to the distance the round barrel merely becomes a rectangular shape that can be created with one polygon.

The small chimney pipes are up high and off in the distance, so they might have an LOD of 1. The clock would have much more detail and thus has an LOD of 4 where the simple shape of the hour hand has an LOD of 1.

Choosing and setting up a set

After you purchase your set, open the Unreal® Engine. Look at the collection of the sets purchased and pick one. We are using a Warehouse set in this example.

Make sure the set is compatible with the Engine version you have.

Now to save it as a Reality™ compatible set.

Go to Edit/Project Settings.

Choose ZDGameMode for the Default (if you don't do this the project will never open in Reality™. Choose the name you just saved WareHouseClass as both the default for the Editor and the Game Map to avoid searching and loading when you open the project.

CLICK ON SAVE ALL.

Creating a storyboard

Now that you have your set you can pre-plan your movie by creating multiple cameras with separate viewpoints to make a storyboard. While not a conventional previz technique involving animation, creating traditional storyboards in this manner is accessible and economical. You can use the Microsoft®

Figure 6.3 *Select Maps and Modes. Screen grab uses the Unreal® Engine. Unreal® is a trademark or registered trademark of Epic Games, Inc. in the United States of America and elsewhere. Unreal® Engine, Copyright 1998–2019, Epic Games, Inc. All rights reserved.*

Windows® 10 "snipping tool" to grab screenshots of your camera views and Adobe® Photoshop® to assemble the images into a storyboard. For simplicity we will make our storyboard using the default ambient lighting for ease of visibility. For a more finished board you can choose to light the environment as demonstrated at the end of this chapter.

Create a camera

Use the red, green, and blue arrows to manipulate the camera position within the set. You can see the view of the camera in the little side window. Be sure to name the camera position as a shot number. Each new position will need you to make a new camera. This becomes like a multi-camera video shoot where you can "cut" to camera 2 etc.

When using the perspective view or camera view in Unreal® the mouse reacts this way.

Left Mouse Button is push in and out.

Right Mouse Button is tilt and rotate.

Middle Mouse Button is up and down.

Figure 6.4 *Go to Cinematic/Cine Camera Actor and click and drag the Cine Camera Actor into the scene. The camera icon with its positional arrows can be seen in the lower right. Screen grab uses the Unreal® Engine. Unreal® is a trademark or registered trademark of Epic Games, Inc. in the United States of America and elsewhere. Unreal® Engine, Copyright 1998–2019, Epic Games, Inc. All rights reserved.*

Figure 6.5 *Use the red, green, and blue arrows to manipulate the camera position within the set. You can see the view of the camera in the little side window. Be sure to name the camera position as shot 1. Each new position will need you to make a new camera. Screen grab uses the Unreal® Engine. Unreal® is a trademark or registered trademark of Epic Games, Inc. in the United States of America and elsewhere. Unreal® Engine, Copyright 1998–2019, Epic Games, Inc. All rights reserved.*

Figure 6.6 *Click on the exit symbol to the left of the Pilot active camera to go back to Perspective view to see the camera itself and easily move it to another location. Once there, you can switch back to camera view to fine tune the position. Screen grab uses the Unreal® Engine. Unreal® is a trademark or registered trademark of Epic Games, Inc. in the United States of America and elsewhere. Unreal® Engine, Copyright 1998–2019, Epic Games, Inc. All rights reserved.*

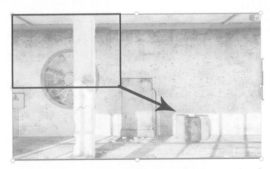

Figure 6.7 *Use the snipping tool or other software to do screen grabs of camera positions to build a storyboard of shots. The red box shows the selection process of the snip. Each camera view should display at the same aspect ratio and size to make the storyboard panels consistent with one another.*

Figure 6.8 *To insert people you can take stills of stand-ins in the approximate pose and camera position as indicated by your set shots, or sketch in a person using Photoshop®. Another option could be the use of stock images that have built-in masks for easy insertion into a storyboard. I personally find it more inspirational to work with actors or models to help capture the mood instead of using generic imagery.*

Once you get a camera angle you like. Use the snipping tool to drag a box around the camera view and save as shot 1, 2, etc. The camera view box will insure that the aspect ratio and size is the same for all screen grabs.

Making a storyboard in Photoshop®

Open Adobe® Photoshop® software and Create New Letter Blank Document.

Figure 6.9 *Open one of the camera position screen grabs then drag it off the shelf using the move tool then select the image and drag it onto the blank letter file image. Adobe® product screenshot(s) reprinted with permission from Adobe®.*

Open one of the images of your live actor in the appropriate pose for that section of the storyboard and drag and drop that image on top of the camera image using the move tool as you did before. Use the corner controls to shrink and position the figure image on top of the background.

Figure 6.10 *Once you have a rough position use the magic wand tool to select the green area and hit the delete button. Adobe® product screenshot(s) reprinted with permission from Adobe®.*

Figure 6.11 *Once the green is removed you can fine tune the position of the figure. If you don't have a green screen you can also trace around a figure using the polygonal lasso tool to eliminate the figure's background. Once all the panels have been positioned and composited save as a Photoshop® file with all the images and then go to Layers/Flatten Image and save as a jpeg image for easy hard-copy printing.*

The Intruder

Figure 6.12 *A storyboard created using screen grabs of the various camera positions in Unreal® combined with Photoshop® placement of the actors in the set to create a poor man's previz storyboard. The first three panels (top to bottom) indicate a pan and push through the window is needed. Once camera 1 is connected to the live-action camera, this push-through shot can easily be accomplished once the live-action tracked camera takes over during the shoot. In the last few panels we see that a character runs through a doorway and shuts and opens a door. As the door is not physically there, we will need to move the door with animation.*

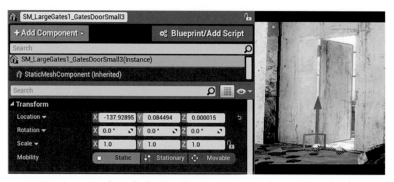

Figure 6.13 *As we go through the Warehouse, we can click on objects within the scene such as this doorway that is ajar. If we open the details of the Door, we can see that the door is hinged and can be moved by moving it on the Z axis. The door can be animated in Reality™ during the shoot. We can also override the camera tracking and have the virtual camera take over and move high up into the sky for dramatic effect if needed. Screen grab uses the Unreal® Engine. Unreal® is a trademark or registered trademark of Epic Games, Inc. in the United States of America and elsewhere. Unreal® Engine, Copyright 1998–2019, Epic Games, Inc. All rights reserved.*

Lighting in Unreal®

For complete flexibility set the light to be a Moveable object. This insures that you will have dynamic lighting effects that react when the light moves or when objects move in front of the light. The choice of Static means that the shadows and lighting will be "baked in" much like painting shadows on a wall. They look good but can't interactively change.

Figure 6.14 *Start with no lights and view the perspective in unlit mode so that you see the set entirely flat lit so you can decide where might be good placements for lights. Screen grab uses the Unreal® Engine. Unreal® is a trademark or registered trademark of Epic Games, Inc. in the United States of America and elsewhere. Unreal® Engine, Copyright 1998–2019, Epic Games, Inc. All rights reserved.*

Figure 6.15 *Go to Lights and drag a point light into an area of the Warehouse. Screen grab uses the Unreal® Engine. Unreal® is a trademark or registered trademark of Epic Games, Inc. in the United States of America and elsewhere. Unreal® Engine, Copyright 1998–2019, Epic Games, Inc. All rights reserved.*

Figure 6.16 *Check all perspective views in wireframe mode to make sure the light is not accidentally imbedded in a wall or something. This could cause Z fighting or confusion in the system leading to blinking objects or odd lights, etc. Screen grab uses the Unreal® Engine. Unreal® is a trademark or registered trademark of Epic Games, Inc. in the United States of America and elsewhere. Unreal® Engine, Copyright 1998–2019, Epic Games, Inc. All rights reserved.*

Figure 6.17 *I positioned the light behind a pillar to cast moody shadows. I tend to place lights where a cinematographer might place them in a real-world setting. In this case behind the pillar so we don't see the light. Even though Unreal® can have the light in the scene without seeing it (impossible in the real world) it can create an odd rendition that departs from the photo-real. You must click on Build Lighting each time you make an adjustment to save the new lighting arrangement. Screen grab uses the Unreal® Engine. Unreal® is a trademark or registered trademark of Epic Games, Inc. in the United States of America and elsewhere. Unreal® Engine, Copyright 1998–2019, Epic Games, Inc. All rights reserved.*

Figure 6.18 *The myriad of lighting controls that change the color temperature, how far the light radiates, the intensity, etc. In this case the point light has a warm color temperature to contrast with the fill to follow. 3200 Kelvin is the color temperature of tungsten lights. In this case we can slightly deviate from that much easier than the cinematographer's tool set of lighting gels. Also note that it is better to have the light be Movable instead of the shown Stationary selection in order to make the light more interactive. After adjusting the point light, I dropped a Sky Light anywhere into the scene. Since this is overall ambient illumination the position is not critical. I adjusted it for a pleasing intensity and bluish color to match the windows for the Warehouse interior. Screen grab uses the Unreal® Engine. Unreal® is a trademark or registered trademark of Epic Games, Inc. in the United States of America and elsewhere. Unreal® Engine, Copyright 1998–2019, Epic Games, Inc. All rights reserved.*

Figure 6.19 *After setting the light you must click on Build Lighting (as shown in Figure 6.17) to have the system recognize the new light arrangement.*

At this point you will have several cameras at a variety of positions within the set that match the storyboard pictures. You have also lit the set. In traditional motion-picture photography, we use one camera and move it about and adjust the lights for each set-up to enhance a close-up, etc. I would encourage the filmmaker to do the same to keep the feeling cinematic. If the scene is lit to satisfy all the camera positions at once, one tends to have a very flatly lit and dull set. Finessing the lighting as you shoot each camera position when you composite the live action is a good practice. Now that we have lit the scene with virtual light let's examine how best to light the live action for compositing.

Chapter 7

Compositing fundamentals

Lighting the live action

In the previous chapter's lighting example, it was a good simulation of how sets are traditionally lit. You get an idea, place the light, and examine the shadows and highlights. You then adjust the light position until it gives just the right effect to help advance the story. When filmmakers start lighting live-action actors on a green cyclorama that simple idea goes out the window because now it seems it's all about the green. We must always keep in mind that the green is not there, it is not the subject, and the objective is to "properly" light the performer so that they fit into the lighting of the set. The practice of flat lighting everything on a green set is mostly due to the prior difficulty of pulling keys off the subject. If one lit everything with flat even light, the key would be great but the composite would still be terrible because the lighting would seldom, if ever, match the background.

Perspective match

In a typical composite the best procedure is to shoot the background image first and take detailed notes of the lens used, height, distance, and tilt of the camera, along with lighting angles, key and fill ratio, color temperature, type of film used, etc. These notes are then used to set up the camera and lights in the same way on the blue or green-screen stage to shoot the foreground element. The green screen was placed several feet away and lit separately to have the proper intensity and saturation. The foreground was shot last as, being a green screen, it was in most cases under controlled stage conditions. There were occasions when the green-screen foreground was shot first, and that often caused issues as the subject was lit without consideration of matching anything and it was quite difficult to shoot a background that matched exactly as many backgrounds were exterior locations where one had to deal with the uncertainties of weather and time of day. It was tempting to "just shoot it" (meaning the foreground green screen) without a reference and thereby potentially locking in a lighting or perspective mismatch. On many occasions a stock background might be purchased with no record of how it was shot. The green-screen cinematographer would then have to estimate the perspective and light direction. In those cases, it was very helpful to make use of a video switcher to do a rough composite on set in order to judge the lighting and perspective. Perspective match is always challenging but made easier if there are basic squared-off forms in the shot such as a table or even a building. With a table one can easily see how much of the top is seen and how the length of the table gets foreshortened. A zoom lens with variable focal length is best used

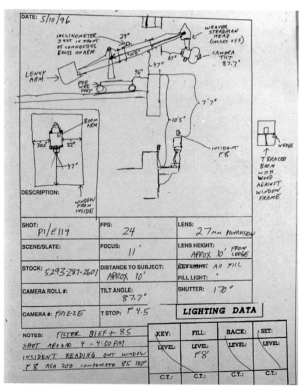

Figure 7.1 *Traditional data sheet as an aid to matching the perspective and lighting of a composite element.*

to find a match by compositing similar forms like apple boxes next to a table in the background image. The lens focal length, height, and tilt of the camera is adjusted until the apple boxes appear to be correct alongside the table. Another test of perspective is to have a stand-in walk toward and away from the camera to see how their image grows and shrinks in relation to the background image. Using an extremely wide focal length may have the figure seem to fit at one distance but as they move forward or back, they may grow and shrink too much and ruin the illusion.

Lighting match

Matching lighting is a bit easier, especially if a floor or ground plane is in the shot. Many times, cinematographers are called painters with light, which is an apt description but often the cinematographer looks to the shadows to match the lighting and not the light itself. The quickest way to match lighting direction is to look at the shadow cast on the floor in the background image and raise, lower, and angle the key light until the shadow of the live-action performer on the green screen matches the length and direction of the shadows on the background. If the floor is not visible then one looks at the shadows and modeling on the subject to match the background appearance.

The second most important match is the key to fill ratio or the contrast. Once again, a rough on-set composite is most helpful in this regard. You will want to match the blackest shadows first and then look to the ratio between the highlights and mid-tones until the contrast matches. If the background plate has an image of people and your foreground is a person, it becomes a much easier situation. The above techniques worked best with locked off camera situations where the variables were limited. In the case of a virtual stage where the green-screen camera is matched perfectly with its virtual counterpart, the perspective match becomes a non-issue. The lighting match method remains the same but now has transformed into more of a real-time all-encompassing lighting situation like normal set photography where both the lighting on the virtual set can be adjusted in tandem with the live-action lighting to get both the real and the virtual to blend perfectly when composited in real time. In that case, the lighting is displaced in space and time between set and performers instead of all together as on a live-action movie set. Time is needed to render the virtual light or bake in the effect on the virtual set while the live-action light adjustment is instantaneous. Some techniques are being developed where lights are tracked like cameras to simultaneously adjust lighting in both the real and virtual locations, but for now it remains a one-at-a-time procedure. Unlike cameras, virtual lights and real lighting instruments are vastly different in how they create lighting on a subject. A virtual light is a mathematical simulation that can be made to illuminate a subject but not cast a shadow, which is impossible with a real light.

Green exposure and technical considerations

The ideal exposure of the green backing is one that allows for the greatest color saturation at an intensity that equals the green level of a properly exposed white board. In other words, the green must hit a sweet spot that has the greatest separation between green and the other primary colors of red and blue without becoming overexposed and clipping. This brightness level would be just enough so that a chicken-wire fence could be easily seen against the screen without overexposure bloom making the delicate wire disappear. For saturation, the best solution is to use the Composite Components green-screen fabric developed by John Erland that has become the motion picture industry standard for green screens (https://digitalgreenscreen.com).

The digital cameras used must have any detail generators turned off so as not to introduce false matte lines due to the synthetic sharpening they create. The color space whenever possible should be 4444 meaning that the luminance and color channel analog signals are all sampled at 4 million times a second to create impeccable resolution for a matte pull. In some cases, 422 is acceptable as well.

The screen should be flatly lit plus or minus one-third of a stop and it goes without saying that the subject should not have any green clothing or objects when shot in front of the green screen. These same guidelines hold true for blue and red screens as well. Red is avoided for human subjects due to the amount of red present in skin tone.

Using the waveform monitor for exposure evaluation

Monitors such as the TV Logic Multi-format LCD Monitor LVM-171WP not only accepts a variety of signals but also has built-in waveform and vector scope monitors. For blue and green screens, the three main goals for the screen are evenness, exposure, and color purity. For digital cameras the best practice is to use the digitalgreenscreen.com fabric lit with tungsten light. A wide spectrum source such as tungsten is better for video and digital while a single limited wavelength source such as pure blue light illuminating the screen is better suited to film. You can use a waveform monitor to check both exposure and evenness. A standard waveform monitor has many markings. The most important of these for the cinematographer is the actual video signal or image that resides in the space between 7.5 to 100 IRE units. Video "black" is represented by 7.5 and the brightest white by 100. A good placement for the green exposure would be a flat even line along the 80 IRE level. If it goes higher or lower than that level it will become more challenging to pull a key. An evenly lit screen will be a straight horizontal line along the 80 IRE mark. If the line dips down on one side, it means that the screen has gotten dark in that area. The waveform can be set to check the evenness from top to bottom as well.

The vector scope

A waveform monitor measures the luminance of a video signal while the vector scope measures the chrominance (the hue and saturation of color) in a video signal. The graticule on this instrument has specific markings for placing the color components of a video color bar test signal. The blue bar signal should rest right in the middle of the B box on the vector scope, the green signal should rest in the middle of the G box. When shooting a green or blue screen the hue and saturation of the screens should come close to these color bar positions. If the color of your screen is spiking toward any other color, you might not have enough purity in your screen.

In Figure 7.2 we see the image of our dog Kona in front of a Composite Components Green Screen designed to work well in outdoor daylight conditions as in this example. The video waveform monitor in the upper right shows that a good exposure of the green screen lies at the 80 IRE level just below peek white. The Gamma Density system 3CP invented by Yuri Newman has its waveform monitor at the lower left meant for high dynamic range imagery and displays the green area between 400 and 500. There is more room above to accommodate highlights such as candle flames and glints. The Vectorscope

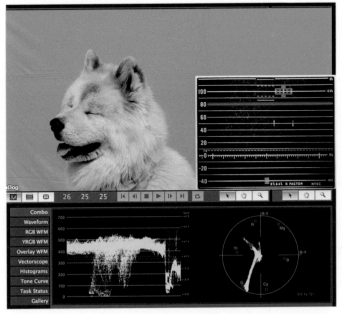

Figure 7.2 *Waveform and Vectorscope monitor displays of a well-lit green screen.*

at the lower right shows the purity of the screen by displaying a spike that extends directly to the G box. When the SMPTE color chart is measured on this scope there will be a star pattern that hits each of the main color boxes. The purity of this screen matches the green reference signal of the SMPTE color chart. If the green screen was pale or desaturated the spike would be much shorter like the spike rising in between the yellow and red coordinates that indicates the lesser color saturation of our dog's fur.

Log or linear

These two terms refer to numbering systems that are used to define the range of tones in an image from black to white. The dynamic range of brightness outside in the real world is huge where the sun is 20,000 times brighter than a black card. To our eye the most important part of that range of light is the area between a white card reflecting about 90% of the light that hits it and a black card. White areas above the brightness of the white card are called super whites and are composed of flames, glints, and of course the sun itself. The numbering problem comes in when one considers that the "sweet spot" between the black and white card takes up a mere 10% of the huge range of light between the sun and black. This 10% is captured quite well with video and linear numbering systems that resolve a 100 to 1 dynamic range. That's why cell phone pictures can look surprisingly good though bright skies often clip to white and lose detail (no fluffy clouds just white sky). The film and digital cinema medium can capture 1,000 to 1 dynamic range meaning they can see into those super whites. It also gives a great deal of wiggle room during color correction. A raw digital file looks flat and washed out because it represents the same appearance as a low-contrast film negative except that it is a positive image. The film negative and raw files are low in contrast to capture the wide dynamic range of light that occurs in nature to enable us to choose the best range (seeing into the shadows or the bright sky) to create the final image in normal contrast for final viewing. Using the log numbering system with high dynamic range images allows for more even distribution of the tones between the white and black card and the super whites so that more of the data is used for the 10% of the most important part of the image. Linear numbering systems by their nature give short shrift to the important 10% section of the dynamic range if they include the 90% section of super whites.

I want the best!

Producers and directors always demand the best, with the producers wanting the best as inexpensively as possible. It is common to be confused and swayed by the technical advertising hype and blurt out I want it all at 8K and 10-bit log! With systems like game engines and live compositing such demands might be feasible if one had access to enough hardware firepower but the cost would be prohibitive. Camera data easily adapts to log capture but computer graphics in a game engine are far more comfortable working in linear space. Blending log and linear images always require that you convert one to the other so that you are combining apples to apples as it were. As an example, blending an 8-bit linear digital matte painting with a log image is horribly difficult if not impossible as the tones never match up. The linear file would need to be converted to log, composited with the log live action and then the final composite turned back to linear for the final presentation. The power of a game engine working in real time is the idea that innumerable computational short-cuts are made that allow real-time rendering and movement. This happens in linear space and is best blended with linear video imagery. If one wants real time and the highest quality possible the best option is to use linear signals out of the camera to combine in real time with the linear output of the game engine while recording the raw camera data in log. Unreal® is capable of outputting the computer graphic in real time in several formats such as 1080p 24 frames per second in real time to match the cameras video output. If both the computer graphic and the raw camera output are recorded separately then they can be recombined in post for maximum quality. The on-set composite then becomes a sophisticated previz that is used as a guide for the final composite. The game engine can render high dynamic range versions of the graphic using the ACES protocol that allows for display on current systems and those into the future. The ACES system essentially created data numbers that include the entire range of human vision beyond the scope of current display devices. When we have display devices that can match human vision ACES has placeholders waiting to be used. In this author's opinion I would stick with straight off-the-shelf high-definition capture and compositing in linear space as both the computer graphics and the green-screen live action are created in highly controlled lighting environments. These systems are primarily designed for live on the air broadcast applications and the final output is quite acceptable for many projects. As filmmakers adopt these systems for production, I am confident that clever pipelines will be created to generate high fidelity imagery in production and post. For those who would like to delve deeply into understanding log and linear concepts above and beyond my extremely truncated explanation, I highly recommend *Digital Compositing for Film and Video* (2nd edition) by Steve Wright (Focal Press, 2006).

The problem of shadows

Pulling shadows from a blue or green screen has always been a daunting challenge. In the past, colored screens were placed 15 or 20 feet away from the subject and only covered the performance area of the subject to reduce or eliminate spill from the screen. This method along with good exposure allowed for superior composites especially if the subject's feet were out of frame. The ability to light the screen separately from the subject was a great advantage. If the actors needed to be seen with their feet touching the floor the best solution (used to this day) was to build a real floor so that the separate lighting scheme for screen and foreground could be followed. This allowed for any type of lighting on the foreground (FG) from high key to dramatic shadow-filled lighting. As time went by however and the compositing tools got better with real-time results, the thirst for flexibility and economy came to the forefront and the industry began to place actors in big green coved stages where they stood on green floors and became bathed in green spill. At first glance this would seem an ideal solution except for the fact that this procedure meant that both screen and subject were lit with the same set-up and, because of the needs of compositing, the lighting on the screen became more important than the lighting on the subject. This is tantamount to the tail wagging the dog. We must remember that the needs of the art outweigh the needs of the tech. The result of favoring the screen lighting leads to a very flat-lit foreground that oftentimes will not match the lighting of the background scene. If the background is shot at sundown with long dark shadows, a foreground element that is lit flatly (to accommodate the screen) will look completely out of place. This is OK for a weather person on a news set but inappropriate for a film. The other issue that occurs is that it is very difficult to pull a good shadow that is falling on a green floor. If the entire screen and subject is lit with a single key light it would be possible to pull an inky black shadow off the screen as the blackness of the shadow becomes much like the blackest part of the subject. If fill light is added, however, we find that the composite struggles as now the shadow becomes a poorly lit portion of the green screen and tends to be extremely noisy, grainy, and nervous, calling undue attention to itself. Often the only solution is to crank up the controls so that the shadow disappears all together, leaving not only a harshly edged subject but one that floats atop the scene with no connection to the environment whatsoever.

Prior solutions

The cleanest solutions to surrounding the subject with green involves no shadow pull at all. In this case the subject is placed on a raised stage far from the screen as is customary but stands on a Mylar or mirrored floor that reflects the green screen and the subject. It is an elegant solution as there is no green spill on the subject, the subject can be lit appropriately, and a clean composite can be made. The problem was that, if not called for, the actor's reflection would have to be painted out and there was no shadow that was cast. In cases of need- ing a shadow the compositor would take the mask of the subject generated by the keying software and use it as a separate element that could be distorted and transformed to appear to lie on the ground in relation to the subject.

Figure 7.3 *The mirror floor technique is extremely effective as it re-uses the flat lighting of the screen for a perfect blend of the wall and floor of the screen while eliminating green spill and allowing the figure to be lit properly. In this case the mirror is an inexpensive silver shiny board on foam core.*

This "false shadow" could then be made soft and as opaque or transparent as needed. Unfortunately, if the subject should walk about it would require a huge amount of effort to align this fake shadow with the subject's legs. If the alignment fails, the illusion is compromised.

Another method of creating a false shadow relies on using virtual light. In this case when the performer is keyed off the green screen (without a shadow) his or her image is placed on a clear polygon plane aligned with the three-dimensional background environment's ground layer. A virtual light is then directed toward what amounts to a paper doll cut-out of the actor, and casts a shadow onto the set. Once again, the softness and transparency of this shadow can be adjusted as well. An example of this is demonstrated in Chapter 9.

The most successful remedy for the shadow problem was the use of a clean plate. In this practice the camera is locked down so no movement can be executed. A clean plate is then shot of the screen by itself with no subject. After the clean plate is photographed the actor comes in and his or her performance is recorded. During the compositing phase the clean plate is put into the keyer as a reference to let the system know what is the subject with their shadow and what is a wrinkle on the green screen. The results of this method created perfectly resolved shadows and excellent composites. The big drawback was the need to have the camera locked down or to use motion-controlled cameras so that a take of a move on the clean plate would exactly match the same move made on the performer against the green. Each frame of a move would have a companion clean plate frame to compare against. This brilliant system was first devised by the Ultimatte Corporation.

Matching lighting with hard shadows

While the clean plate helps tremendously with resolving shadows, the lighting must match between the subject and the background. With harsh film noir lighting this need not be challenging if you isolate the areas of green screen and light them properly. In this example we need to have an even green screen on the back wall but need to have hard sharp shadows on the foreground subject. Having too much fill light on a hard-key subject defeats the "look" of the image. If you have a subject that has only a key light and no fill it is perfectly acceptable to have a green-screen floor raised and far from the green wall so that it can be lit solely by the key light at enough distance to diminish hot spots. The larger and farther the key is from the floor, the more evenly lit it will be. Light the back wall separately to match the intensity of the floor and both the green floor and wall will blend together. A raised green floor is much better than a cove as the one plane of green floor will seamlessly blend with the green wall at the far edge of the raised stage. A cove by its nature almost always generates a hot spot somewhere along the curvature. Using the raised stage floor method, even dramatic lighting can be used with green composites without having to resort to extreme post processing to create false contrast.

Figure 7.4 *The overall flat lighting method allows for the resolution of real shadows with a moving camera but if the lighting remains flat the composite will fail as this real shadow will not match the background lighting. Courtesy of Mobile Motion MoCap.*

Figure 7.5 *To light the scene properly a single hard key source is used to cast a one-directional shadow. This light also serves to evenly light the floor of the screen using reduced fill. The fixtures used to light the back wall are pushed back so as not to interfere with the subject lighting. Courtesy of Mobile Motion MoCap.*

Figure 7.6 *When hard foreground lighting is blended with soft back wall lighting proper shadow effects can be produced. The key light height and angle is adjusted while watching the shadow and comparing it to shadows in the background using the composite image. Courtesy of Mobile Motion MoCap.*

Zero Density and the Reality Engine™ system

Building upon the prior art we find that the Reality™ system, along with modern motion tracking tools such as Mo-Sys, allows for effortless recreation of shadows off a green environment. The Reality™ system rides atop the Unreal® Game Engine in order to incorporate 3D compositing within the CG environment. 3D compositing differs from 2D as it is not merely one image layer placed on top of another as in traditional methods but one that places the keyed performer within the 3D space itself. In this case our paper doll cut-out can walk behind and in front of the dimensional objects within the game set using projection methods. The compositing system also allows freedom of camera movement when coupled with a camera tracker such as Mo-Sys that links to a virtual camera. The tremendous advantage of this linking is that a synthetic

Figure 7.7 *The foreground subject now fits in with the lighting of the set. In an ideal situation, the floor the actor is on should be a raised platform of green with completely isolated lighting from the far back wall, avoiding the necessity of using a cove at all. Safety considerations and economy, however, have made coves the norm. Courtesy of Mobile Motion MoCap.*

copy of the green-screen cove is also made and superimposed over the same virtual space that the real screen would have occupied in the CG set. So now instead of using motion control to do a move on a clean plate for one take and another take with the identical move for the performer to be composited later, the Reality Engine™ system does this combination instantly and on the fly. Real shadows are preserved frame-by-frame as the camera moves because the image of the clean plate keeps up with the image of the live-action performer against green. The live-action camera records the actor against green and the virtual camera records the clean plate of green along with the background alone. After compositing we have an excellent composite that preserves transparencies and shadows. The only thing the cinematographer must keep in mind is to pull back and record the clean plate image of the green screen whenever there is a change of lighting. Doing so will update the image of the screen on top of the virtual copy of the green cove created within the CG set. In practice it is best to once again keep the background screen 15 to 20 feet away from the subject and have a raised green floor where both the performer and green floor are lit for the aesthetics of the story. In a hard-key scenario, it is best to have a powerful spot some distance away from the green floor to not only light the area evenly but also to avoid the pitfalls of the inverse square law where areas close to the light are much brighter than areas further away. Having a light far away greatly reduces or eliminates this effect. The fill can then be adjusted accordingly. As long as the clean plate is shot, we can once again create aesthetically pleasing composites with proper shadows that don't interfere or call attention to the shot but blend seamlessly so as not to distract from the story.

Chapter 8
Production considerations

Point of view

Throughout literary history there have been several points of view when telling a story. Omniscient author where the storyteller knows everything about the characters and relates that knowledge to the audience is quite popular. Other points of view would be first person or the speaker (I), second person or the person spoken to (you), and finally the third person or person spoken about (he/she).

In the visual language of movies, the camera recording the action is often the omniscient author giving a "God's eye" visual point of view to the story. While this type of viewer can be anywhere within the scene as a spectator, we often limit the number of views to prevent confusion when watching the movie. The limit of the number of views is based on how an audience views a play when watching a performance under the proscenium arch. The audience member views the scene looking at the front of the stage and is not expected to get out of their seat, go on stage and look at the play from behind the stage (unless they are downright rude and want to get ejected from the theater). This gave rise to the 180-degree rule where the camera never crosses the eyeline between characters after a cut to keep the spatial relationship left to right etc. in continuity.

When I went to film school in the 70s, I remember one of my instructors taking issue with compositions that have the camera placed within a burning fireplace to view the action. "What are we doin' in the fireplace?" he would say. It gives one pause to think as it takes some people out of the story by focusing on the techniques of cinema rather than the story. In this case the perceived God's eye view becomes more of the invisible mortal's eye view, who is in danger of burning up! On the other hand, shots like this can be very intriguing and bring added meaning to a story if the character is reading from an occult book for example and the fireplace symbolizes their descent into the pit of hell.

High vantage points gave rise to magnificent shots in movies but were often limited to the height that a movie crane could achieve. When shooting miniatures, the basic rule of thumb was to place the camera where it would be if the miniature was full size. In other words, we would avoid shooting from high up as normally a live-action camera wasn't able to be placed 300 feet in the air unless on a helicopter. If a miniature is shot from high up, much scrutiny is placed on the model making it look like a toy.

Today's point of view

With the amazing advancements in drone technology and the miniaturization of cameras we find that our point of view (POV) can truly be anywhere. One popular convention today is to shoot a spokesperson from the wings of the stage as it were where we see them in profile speaking to the audience off camera rather than directly to the camera. The Steadicam allows for smooth continually gliding moves throughout the scene replicating theater in the round or being allowed to be on the stage itself. With the advent of virtual reality (VR) headsets the spectator determines the POV. Basically, we are in

Figure 8.1 *"What are we doin' in the fireplace?"*

an exciting time of invention with POV and the ways in which we tell stories. The rules are being broken all the time to brilliant or ill effect. In the case of our virtual backlot, however, where we are compositing live action with a synthetic set, we must adhere to the rule of station point if we are to avoid on-set compositing problems.

Station point

In compositing where one combines several different photographic elements it is important to use the same lens, camera tilt angle, F-stop, focus, lighting, and station point (where the camera is placed in relation to the subject) for every element so that they can be combined seamlessly. While the tracking system and Reality™ system appear to do this for you automatically except for the lighting, one must be aware of height issues.

In a typical VR stage we are limited by how high or low the camera can go without special construction.

In this VR stage shown in Figure 8.2 we have a truss supporting the 36 Qualysis mocap cameras for capture of motion within the stage. The camera jib can raise

Figure 8.2 *A typical range of camera motion in a VR stage. Courtesy of Mobile Motion MoCap.*

and lower the camera and can also dolly in and out and zoom. We must keep in mind that this stage is always at ground level when realizing extreme up or down angles.

In this example the live camera views the mocap performer for compositional reference while tracking information is sent to the system to move the virtual camera and the synthespian inside the set as shown in the monitor below. This pipeline uses a camera tracker to stream information into the Unity Game Engine. Note the time delay as the live performer claps his hands while the synthespian is processed a few frames behind in the image above.

Camera station points

The uppermost image of Figure 8.3 shows where a traditional cinematographer might place their camera if this was a real warehouse, shooting up at the top of the staircase to capture the action.

If this camera placement is used in a game engine it will be fine for the set image, but not the live-action extension of this camera because it will be at the ground plane facing the green screen. If the live-action camera tilts up this far it will miss the actors entirely unless they are raised to the same height as the

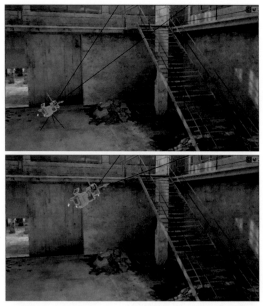

Figure 8.3 *Anticipating constricted camera placement on the VR stage when choosing camera positions in the previz. Screen grab uses the Unreal® Engine. Unreal® is a trademark or registered trademark of Epic Games, Inc. in the United States of America and elsewhere. Unreal® Engine, Copyright 1998–2019, Epic Games, Inc. All rights reserved.*

synthetic staircase. It would also call for the green screen to be placed above their heads.

The bottom image shows a better placement of the Unreal® camera for ease of shooting the live action on the subsequent VR stage. By raising the synthetic camera to obtain a much more workable tilt angle, the live action becomes much easier to match the station point. The live-action camera on a boom arm can be placed very close to the floor to obtain a less extreme tilt angle and the actors can be placed higher using green boxes that align to the floor of the synthetic set. While standing on green boxes will work with the keyer, one must keep in mind that the virtual cyclorama will not have virtual green boxes and therefore the "clean plate" may not work as effectively in the area of the green boxes and may require post compositing to refine the work.

Cheating the subject

In cases where the actor is willing to work with a compromise in gravity, certain low-angle shots looking up at an actor can be done by placing the performer on apple boxes or a bench that will support him or her in front of the green screen at an extreme angle while the live camera shoots across their torso

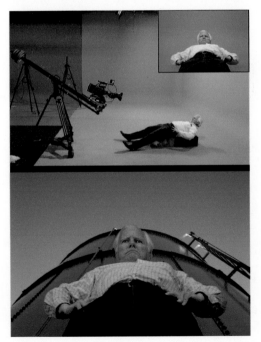

Figure 8.4 *To avoid the hassle of placing a green screen on the ceiling for extreme up-shots, one can re-orient co-operative talent to achieve the same effect in an expeditious manner. Courtesy of Mobile Motion MoCap.*

directly toward the screen. The Unreal® set position is then adjusted to offset the view to accommodate the easier placement of the production camera.

Extreme camera moves

One great advantage of the virtual cyclorama system is that the green screen itself not only becomes a key for the actors, but the area of the screen becomes its own garbage matte that cuts out everything outside of the screen area to hide the grips, lights, etc. to eliminate the need for post processing. This means that the camera can rotate 360 degrees to encompass the entire virtual set while compositing live action within the screen area. If the camera jib can only go so high, the synthetic camera can hook-up and override the live camera and rise hundreds of feet in the air above the virtual set.

Using a header to expand the green-screen area

There are occasions when the built-in garbage matte idea will fail. One example is when a performer enters from the camera position and fills the frame as he walks into the green stage. In order to avoid having the top of his body cut off by the garbage matte, or needing extensive hand-drawn matte creation, we must economically add to the green area. This is done with a header or a drape of green suspended from above that will cover the actor at the beginning

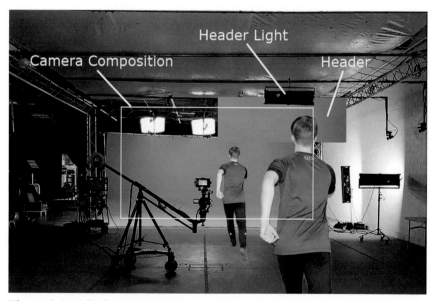

Figure 8.5 *A header can increase the area of the green screen even with a low ceiling. For purposes of illustration, the header does not cover the entire top of the frame as it normally would. Courtesy of Mobile Motion MoCap.*

of the shot and yet be high enough so that the actor can walk beneath it as he or she steps into the stage. In cases like this special consideration will need to be made as to how to handle the clean plate as a header is not included in the generic cyclorama mesh.

Motion-capture considerations

We have entered into an amazing new age of actors being able to interact with fantastic creatures and characters generated by the computer and controlled by motion-capture technology. If intimate interactive performance is needed where the human performer looks at the mocap performer within the same frame, one must be aware that the CG character generated may not be able to "cover up" the mocap actor perfectly, especially if there are large variations in anatomy. A mocap actor's arms for example can never be as long as an ape's arms so would require a good deal of post compositing to erase the mocap actor from the scene. In cases where mocap actors are in a real set alongside the human characters, it is best to shoot a clean plate of the set without performers to make the work in post much easier when erasing and inserting CG characters. Any intimate touching such as shaking hands is particularly difficult and would be best accomplished by having the mocap actor have a special character

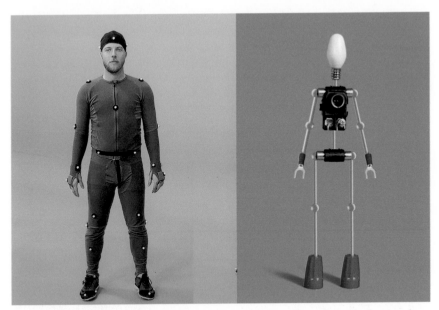

Figure 8.6 *Very often the anatomy of mocap performers will not fit inside the virtual characters' anatomy, which can preclude the mocap performer and the live performer appearing alongside each other in the same shot for a live output. If anatomy is mismatched, the mocap actor must perform outside the view of the live-action camera unless a lot of post-production work is planned for. Courtesy of Mobile Motion MoCap.*

Figure 8.7 *Tape is used to establish eyelines for the two performers in a mirror shot so they appear to look at each other. The image below shows the final composite. From* Mirror Magic: Visual Effects Using Reflections *by Mark Sawicki (DVD). "Mirror Magic" course images courtesy of Stan Winston School of Character Arts.*

glove that matches the anatomy and texture of the synthetic character to allow for the two characters to actually touch in that region of the hand where the rest of the synthetic character is blended at the wrist to complete the illusion.

For live performance it is best to create scenarios where there is no physical contact and to keep the mocap performer in a separate area from the performers in front of the green screen. Monitors are used to allow the actors to see the composite so that they can adjust their eyelines and performances. There is nothing new here as older traditional methods such as Pepper's ghost mirror effects required actors to work in this way.

Be prepared for back lighting

Normally an on-the-spot decision to introduce an extremely bright back light is seldom an issue unless it involves a green backing for a composite. When

Figure 8.8 *As with the mirror shot, the mocap area is separate from the green-screen area. Monitors allow the actors to gauge their performance allowing for seamless compositing without the need for post. Courtesy of Mobile Motion MoCap.*

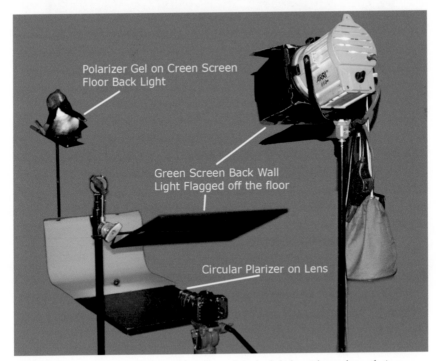

Figure 8.9 *Putting a polarizing gel in front of the back light with another polarizer on the lens will knock out the glare.*

Figure 8.10 *Using polarizers on light and lens will eliminate floor glare and some specular reflections off the subject and will enable a quality composite.*

one back lights on a green floor, the angle of incidence equals the angle of reflection and you are left with a huge white glare on the floor that becomes a compositing nightmare. The first impulse is to use a polarizing filter on the camera, but this will be of marginal help. The real trick is to put a polarizing gel on the back light and a circular polarizer on the camera lens. Using this arrangement will ensure that the green floor stays green and keep the shadow as well.

Aesthetic blending of composites

There have been remarkable films made using virtual techniques such as *Sin City* (2005) and *300* (2006). In those cases, the live-action elements were modified and enhanced in order to blend well with the graphic nature of the environments. In the case of virtual sets that are "almost" photo-real, we can assist the match of the live-action images by reducing the dynamic range of the live action in post by using a cartoon filter with level adjustments.

Figure 8.11 *Matching the look. In the top image we have a photo-real human composited against a CG environment with limited detail and dynamic range. As it is difficult to increase the detail and resolution of the computer-graphic element, a better match of the look can be had by decreasing the dynamic range and detail of the live action as seen in the bottom image.*

Sound considerations

When working in such a visually oriented technology, short shrift is often given to sound, which is vitally important to any program. Very often the off-hand solution for sound is to give everyone a lavalier microphone that travels with the performer and can be made wireless. While this is a good solution for sound capture, the drawback of this technique is the constant intimacy of the recording as the microphone is always close to the subject. This "presence" is great for close-ups but becomes out of place for wide shots. It is for this reason that professional microphone boom technique is the preferred method for sound recording of narrative movie productions. When two performers are engaged in a conversation, the boom operator adjusts the position of the microphone to favor the one who is speaking and repositions throughout the dialog. If one subject needs to scream during the scene the boom operator is aware and pulls the microphone far away from the subject to attenuate the louder sound. Modifying the sound input by changing the position and distance of a

Figure 8.12 *The Zoom H5 recorder. Image © 2019 ZOOM Corporation. All Rights Reserved.*

microphone from the subjects is the preferred method of "mixing" with the boom as opposed to constantly riding the volume control of the microphone.

A good inexpensive sound recorder is the Zoom H5. A boom pole with a shotgun microphone such as an Audio-Technica AT897 or a BOYA BY-PVM 1000 that have a shock mount, foam windscreen, and fur windshield.

Holding a boom

The hands should be above the shoulders and shoulder-length apart for the best control and least fatigue. The microphone should be at a 90-degree angle to the boom and the boom is kept level. The proper microphone position is to point it at an imaginary cup suspended just below the speaker's chin. When the actor moves so does the boom. The microphone should have both the windscreen and windshield with the low-cut filter turned on to help reduce noise. Make sure all cables are taught and not moving during recording.

Figure 8.13 *Proper posture for holding the boom. Courtesy of Mobile Motion MoCap.*

Recorder set-up

- Set the date and time to match the camera's date and time to make it easier to match sound and picture in editing.
- It is best to not turn on special filters such as comp/limiter to preserve quality. The comp/limiter is used in case gunshots are recorded to engage immediate clamping of the signal. In most cases it is not needed.
- Record in mono.
- The format is typically Wav48khz/24 bit.
- Adjust headphone levels to be barely comfortable (slightly less than too loud) for good monitoring.
- During rehearsal, with the microphone properly positioned, adjust the record level so that the loudest words peak at 60 dB and the quiet words are higher than −18 dB.
- Adjust the microphone as needed during the performance to mix the recording instead of adjusting the recording level on the H5.
- At the end of the scene be sure to record one minute of room tone (the sound of the empty room with no person making a sound) to be used in sound editing to fine tune the scene's audio.

I would like to thank James Coburn, CAS, for sharing these abbreviated tips on proper sound recording for motion pictures.

The next chapter will address the challenge of getting back to the tried and true method of compositing the real with the real in traditional effects work within the constraints and challenges of the virtual environment.

Chapter 9
Creating photo-real environments

While the illusive mystery of locking live-camera movement together with a virtual camera has been solved with live-camera tracking systems, the big challenge is in making the composite photo-real. The computer graphic set is perfect for capturing the infinite number of perspective changes and displacements that occur during regular cinematography as the set is truly three-dimensional and will respond to the lens in the same way, as real three-dimensional objects are perceived by a moving live-action camera. What is difficult to accomplish with CG sets is the photo-real component. It often gets close but always has the uphill battle of fighting the computer's own perfection. One must "dirty up" the data of the CG set to make sure all the lines aren't straight or the surfaces pristine. False dirt is painted on flat planes and cheats are used throughout to keep the render times manageable. The result is great for an interactive video-game world but fails when we are expected to fool the eye into thinking that the live-action actors are really in a live-action environment. One solution is to change the ratio between the real and the synthetic by using "augmented reality." Augmented reality basically places a synthetic character in a live-action environment. Because the character takes up less real estate and computing power more attention can be given toward making the character photo-real. For a virtual backlot composite where human actors inhabit a photo-real virtual set, the solution is to do what has always been done in the past and that is to

Figure 9.1 *A traditional high-quality composite where both the foreground and the background are real photographic elements matched in perspective, lighting, and color.*

Figure 9.2 *An example of augmented reality where mocap performers manipulate CG characters within Unreal® or Unity. The characters and their shadows are composited atop a live-action background in the proper perspective. We still see a pronounced difference in the look of the real background and that of the synthetic appearance of the CG. Courtesy of Mobile Motion MoCap.*

combine the real with the real by making CGI more real through photographic augmentation. The challenge becomes how to turn flat photography into dimensional objects that will change in perspective during camera movement.

The challenge of depth

The easiest solution to have the background photo-real is to shoot several overlapping views of an environment to create a stitched panoramic background that can be mapped onto a large polygonal sphere that is self-illuminating within the game engine. The virtual camera then sits in the middle and pans or dollies about and records the live-action background just like a real camera. Let's say our shot is a ride on a flying carpet. If the carpet is static our live-action camera can pan and tilt to stay with the actors while compositing the clouds and sky in the background. Very little changes in perspective as the horizon and distant mountains are at infinity and no perspective change would happen. If the camera were to dolly forward however the virtual camera would get closer to the textured sphere and the mountains in the distance would get too big too soon just as if we had painted a picture of clouds and mountains in a domed room and the camera moved closer to the wall. This often happens in traditional effects photography where a window is covered with green material that includes tracking targets. If the camera pushes in on the window and the background is tracked to fit exactly on top of the targets, then the background becomes much like a photo glued to the glass rather than being outside the window. In cases like this, the up-down movement is tracked but the size of the background is left alone so that when the camera pushes in, the far distant background doesn't get larger but mimics the infinity distance. In the case of our flying carpet the system could be designed so that as the camera pushes in, the dome pushes away so that the image remains the same size.

Creating dimension with flat imagery

In the 1930s the Walt Disney company achieved a three-dimensional effect in their animated films by using a multi-plane camera. Several layers of artwork were separated by space as a camera pushed past them. The top layer got bigger faster and then the mid layer and so on as they were spaced at different distances from the camera. When the camera moved close enough to clear the art of the top layer that layer was removed so the camera could continue to the next. To prevent an exposure increase resulting from the missing layer a blank glass filter was added in front of the lens so that the exposure remained the same while the camera continued to push in. The technique was used on the film *Pinocchio* (1940) to startling effect. In the case of our virtual set we can do the same thing by placing planes of photographic imagery representing objects at different distances, cut out to reveal imagery beyond such as flat

True Perspective "Dolly" move.

Flattened Perspective "Zoom" effect.

Figure 9.3 *In a true 3D perspective move the mountains stay at infinity and do not have perceptible increase in size. If the image of the mountains stays stuck to the window no perspective change takes place and it mimics the look of a zoom. This can have a "wallpaper" appearance if the live-action camera dollies toward a window but the image outside the window stays stuck to the window frame.*

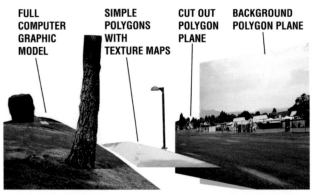

FULL COMPUTER GRAPHIC MODEL

SIMPLE POLYGONS WITH TEXTURE MAPS

CUT OUT POLYGON PLANE

BACKGROUND POLYGON PLANE

Figure 9.4 *One can get away with flat imagery for distant subjects. Objects close to the camera require three-dimensional objects.*

images of boulders in the foreground, and beyond that a hill, and beyond that a mountain. In the virtual world the scale and separation of the flat planes can be adjusted to reproduce a realistic perspective change as the virtual camera dollies forward. Much post work is required since the original photography is two-dimensional and the different distance planes must be cut out of the picture. Once a portion of the flat image is cut out, a large blank space will remain in the original that will need to be filled in and replaced using cloning techniques. As an example, foreground boulders could be cut out from the image for the first plane but then a hole would remain in the image where the boulders were. Through cloning techniques, the empty space left by the cut-out boulders would have to be painted back in so that when we move past the photo boulder in the foreground plane, more of a continuous background beyond will be revealed. This technique is often used in documentary films to enliven and give synthetic dimension to still photographs.

Photos on blocks

A simple but effective method of achieving photo-real dimensional imagery in a miniature was executed by the Skotak brothers for the film *Escape from New York* (1981). A glider was seen wafting past buildings of a darkened New York skyline. The brothers took photo blow-ups of the sides of buildings and glued them to the sides of apple boxes to create the city. The lighting on the dimensional photo buildings would create highlights and shadows as the real buildings would, and the camera would show perspective change. All the details and reality of the buildings came from the glued photos. The exact same thing can be done in the virtual world using polygonal blocks with perhaps modeled ledges and awnings to enhance the dimension. The photography would then be texture-mapped onto the virtual buildings. The trick is to always photograph the building side from a flat perspective and in ambient light with no shadows or bright highlights. This will allow for the virtual light to illuminate the set properly. We will examine this technique in Chapter 10.

Closer and closer the photogrammetry solution

The ultimate solution for photo-real environments would be to create dimensional photographs to fill the virtual space. What I'm referring to is not stereoscopic photography that uses an inter-ocular offset to mimic the perspective seen by the eye but a photograph that has a depth dimension. If we took a photograph of a door it would result in a flat plane that showed the doorknob from one angle. If we moved to the side of that photograph it would be readily apparent that the doorknob is flat and does not protrude from the door. A dimensional photograph would have the doorknob sticking out from the door just as it does in real life. It is essentially a three-dimensional model of a door made from photography. The process to create such a model is called photogrammetry.

In practice, one takes several photographs from a variety of station points. One can either surround an object with many cameras to capture its appearance from many views from this full circle collection of observation points or can conversely have one camera and rotate the object to capture many views of its appearance from all angles. All these photographs are then put into computer software to compare overlapping images to deduce the actual spatial dimension of the object and create a point cloud of an image that essentially creates a photo-realistic dimensional model from a collection of photographs. The more photos you take the more accurate the model becomes. Sounds simple, right? Well the devil is in the detail, and the process will always require a great deal of editing to clean up missing or erroneous data. Some parts of the image may be occluded by a portion of the object itself that will leave drop-outs or gaps in the image such as the top of a person's head may be missing if a head

Figure 9.5 *A series of photographs from different viewpoints of a subject can be computed to create a three-dimensional photo-real object. If all the views are photographed with flat even lighting, then the 3D object can be lit with virtual light to create highlights and shadows.*

is the subject and not enough photographs were taken that included the top of the head.

Polygon framework reduction

Once the software has resolved and created the dimensional photo from many photographs, the image that is now a texture map will rest on top of a polygonal framework. This collection of polygons will be very dense and will need to be trimmed a lot for the computation process to be fast enough for real-time virtual stage work. In the case of a pillar for example one could have an enormous number of striations to create an exceptionally smooth curvature or use just a few to support the texture map. Quite often just a few will do as most of the illusion is coming from the photo itself. The top of the pillar may have ornate carvings of characters and in this case the poly count can remain denser. Flat walls can suffice with a simple plane. This is very similar to the age-old theatrical stage method of stretching canvas on simple wooden frames and painting them to create the illusion of a simple room set. Using photographs in this case yields more realistic results in our virtual stage.

Photo resolution

A compositor is keenly aware of needing to maintain quality by always using elements that match or surpass the final output resolution. As an example, if you were working in high-definition resolution of 1920 × 1080, the images you work with in the composite must be at least that resolution and if you

Figure 9.6 *A 3D model of the Venetian Doge Palace acquired with photogrammetry and rendered in real time with Halide FX by Elliot Mack. Courtesy of Lightcraft.*

intend to push in on the image then its resolution should be 4K or higher so that no degradation of the image occurs.

In the case of photogrammetry, it becomes trickier as you must know what the virtual camera is going to do. If the shot is a static camera angle of two people talking atop a bridge with the city in the background, one would not need photogrammetry at all and a straightforward background video at the output resolution would be fine to map onto a simple polygon. The problem occurs when the camera moves into the scene and gets close to an object within the scene such as a kiosk, phone booth, or the like. One could shoot a high-resolution fisheye of the scene to allow for a push in, but degradation would quickly occur. The trick is to manufacture high-resolution photogrammetry models that sit in space in front of lower resolution backgrounds in the distance. St. Mark's Square in Venice, Italy, for example has buildings supported by dozens of columns that are all unique in and of themselves. Instead of making a photogrammetry model encompassing the entire building from a distance, each column can be photographed up close for a highly detailed view allowing the virtual camera to move extremely close to the pillars without loss of resolution. Halide creator Elliot Mack took 700 photographs of this location and after a month of editing, created a virtual St. Mark's Square as a photogrammetry generated ultra-realistic environment with enough resolution to push in to the delicate details atop the columns.

Lighting issues with outdoor locations

In a perfect-world location, photogrammetry would take place on a cloudy day with many hours of ambient light. One could take time to painstakingly capture the environment from every possible viewpoint with consistent lighting. Since we still cannot control the weather the best option is to be speedy and photograph before or after sunrise at the magic hour. What you risk in photographing in daylight is the possibility of more editing fixes if you can't capture all the shots needed before the sun moves and changes the lighting, but more specifically you will "bake in" the light direction of your models. The baked-in lighting is perfectly acceptable but limits the flexibility a director will have with the virtual location. Having the space created with flat lighting allows for virtual lights to highlight, model, and cast shadows of the photo-textured sets so that they can serve for both daylight and night scenes with total control of key light direction.

Breaking the illusion

If several shots within a scene (such as the St. Mark's Square example) are designed to take place under the arches and beside the pillars of an ancient building and the "stage" is contained within 20–30 feet, then extremely realistic sets and scene will be created. If the director (on a whim) decides to create a steady-cam shot that chases the actor out onto the courtyard right up to the edge of the dock, the reality will break, and the illusion will be destroyed unless detailed photogrammetry models were taken at that part of the location. The "breaking" would appear as the ground appeared as streaks of blurred color and mooring masts were revealed as flat cut-outs and pixelated imagery. There are always limits to every trick. In traditional work, examples of "breaking" would be panning on a foreground miniature when the camera is not on the nodal point resulting in the miniature becoming unregistered with the background or pushing in too far on a rear projection resulting in a blurry image.

Previsualization

For a good workflow when executing the virtual set process, it is extremely helpful for the director to work with a previsualization company to create a full CGI rendition of the scene and shots he or she has in mind. Once this is done, the photogrammetry plate crew can shoot just enough material of the real location in an expeditious manner to allow for straightforward virtual set creation to accommodate the previz.

Ok, we didn't do any of that, now what?

Ah yes, as the real world would have it, things don't always go as planned and we also don't want to restrict our director in a moment of inspiration (unless you're the producer paying for all this). In this case, such as the steady-cam example I mentioned above, you just go ahead and do it and forget what the background looks like. The environment now merely becomes a rough template previz to be "fixed" later. The taking camera's raw data is a picture of our actors in front of a green screen so they can always be composited on an improved synthetic set later. This is also the case with game engine-generated backgrounds that are close to real but not quite there. Once the data of the camera move is collected those same backgrounds can be re-rendered using much longer frame-by-frame rendering tools that can include global illumination, radiosity, and other methods to make the CG models look much more realistic. In the case of photogrammetry, it may require another photo session of the location to collect more data for the areas that broke.

Holographic capture
Traditional laser hologram
The invention of the laser beam allowed for the creation of the first practical hologram in 1962 by Yuri Denisyuk in the Soviet Union and by Emmett Leith and Juris Upatnieks at the University of Michigan.

In this process the beam of a laser is spread and split in two directions. One beam shines and bounces off the subject while the other acts as a reference signal both exposing a high-fidelity film emulsion so that, when combined, it creates an extremely fine interference pattern on the film. Under ordinary light the film just looks like a dull gray blob but when a laser illuminates the surface the object is recreated in full three dimensions and can be viewed in full 360 space. If the photographic film is cut in two, one can still see the entire figure but the number of views becomes limited. As an example, cutting a tiny

Figure 9.7 *Jason Sapan (aka Dr. Laser) holding his large-format transmission hologram taken of a model of a building. Courtesy of Holographic Studios.*

corner of such a hologram would reveal the entire subject from one point of view. The process is difficult to execute as one must float the laser, mirrors, lenses, film, and subject on a vibration-free table to obtain blur-free interference patterns. The size of the film was limited but the process did capture a true three-dimensional reproduction of an object.

Holographic stereogram

This technique was a clever process invented by Lloyd Cross and developed by the School of Holography and the Multiplex company. The process entailed photographing a performer on a rotating pedestal with a motion-picture camera. Jason Sapan, proprietor of Holographic studios, shared this explanation of the process also known as an integral hologram:

> [T]he subject was on a turntable rotating in front of a motion picture camera. Every frame of film goes through the camera at a rate of 24 frames per second. Meanwhile, the rate of rotation of the turntable on which the subject is standing is one and one third rotations per minute. This records one third of a degree of rotation per frame of film. Each frame of film is projected one at a time through an optical printer (like a professional movie projector) and then horizontally compressed through an anamorphic lens that turns the projected film frame into a narrow vertical strip that is holographic recorded by interfering it with a second narrow strip of laser light that is called the reference onto the holographic film. After each horizontally compressed frame of film is recorded onto the holographic film that is mounted on a cylinder, it is rotated a millimeter to allow for the next holographic exposure on this film. This is sequentially produced one frame at a time as the motion picture film advances and the cylinder bearing the holographic film is advanced by a stepping motor (⅓ of one degree if you will of the cylinder). After the sequence of exposures is complete, usually a run of 1,080 frames, the film is taken to a darkroom and processed to create the hologram. As the viewer witnesses the holographic image, their left eye views the image of up to sixty sequentially recorded frames while their right eye views the image of another sixty or so frames that are slightly advanced in the original motion picture film making them horizontally displaced enough to provide a stereoscopic overlap of the subject that frequently can appear to move within the cylinder as it rotates depending upon whether the subject was moving in the 2D film recording.

This resulted in a startling photo-real performer in a glass cylinder effect but was limited in scope and action. These cylinders were quite popular in the 70s and are featured in the film *Logan's Run* (1976).

I want to give special thanks for Mr. Sapan for sharing his imagery and explanation of the process. His unique school and museum are located in Manhattan New York (https://www.holographer.com).

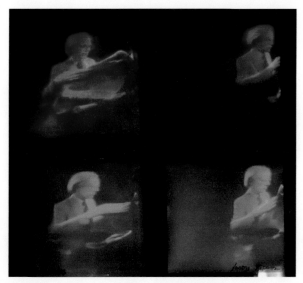

Figure 9.8 *An integral hologram portrait of Andy Warhol created by Jason Sapan in 1977. This particular display shows four different views from the cylinder as a homage to Warhol's style of work made for the Museum of Arts and Design for their biennial. Courtesy of Holographic Studios.*

The light field camera (plenoptic camera)

This brilliant invention had its roots in 1908 when Gabriel Lippman conceived of the integral photography camera that involved an array of lenses placed on top of the film emulsion, much like that of a fly's eye, to capture and record the scene from a variety of different viewpoints crudely replicating with optical means the multi-view recording offered by the laser hologram. For years the concept remained largely dormant until revisited in the 90s. A paper written by Edward H. Adelson and James R. Bergen described a method of representing light in a volume in a 5th-dimensional space. The capture of this light field recorded an enormous number of individual light rays present in a scene enabling miracles such as depth information that allowed for the depiction of perspective shift and refocusing the image after the photograph was taken!

In a 1996 Siggraph presentation Marc Levoy and Pat Hanrahan of Stanford University demonstrated how the dimensional image was reconstructed by showing a close-up of the light field recording where one could see an array of full views of the subject from a large number of individual perspective viewpoints. The two-dimensional slice from the array could depict the full view from one perspective or for a closer view, the 2D slice would be compiled from individual light-ray recordings derived from several of the array images. Unlike a flat panorama the viewer could now see the reproduction of dimension, texture, and glints that we see in real life.

Figure 9.9 *The plenoptic camera. Instead of using many cameras to capture the subject from a variety of viewpoints, a single lens captures the subject as an aerial image within the camera that is then refocused by a micro array of tiny lenses to record a variety of viewpoints onto the sensor. The close-up view of the subject's eye shows the different views captured of the eye from one side to the front to the other side. This information is then used to create a depth map where unique colors indicate the distances of objects from the camera. This tremendous amount of information permits the user to focus the image after the fact, as shown at the bottom of the illustration, as well as creating a true 3D representation of the scene. Courtesy of the Raytrix GmbH company (www.raytrix.de).*

In 2006 Ren Ng a Stanford researcher founded the Lytro company that set about its mission to create consumer-available light field cameras. One of their first cameras used a standard lens focusing the image on an array of microlenses atop the sensor to record a limited-view light field that allowed for post focusing and a limited perspective view of a couple of inches. The company went on to develop the Immerge camera that was able to scan a location and record a much larger light field area allowing the viewer to see a photo-real reproduction of how we see the world with a tremendous number of constantly changing viewpoints. The camera was costly, and the scan required about 30 seconds to capture the light field of a room, but the results were spectacular. Lytro ceased operations in March 2018, having been purchased by Google. Currently the Raytrix company founded in 2009 offers cameras and services in light field capture.

Paul Debevec, senior staff engineer at Google VR and adjunct research professor at USC's Institute for Creative Technology, continued research in this field developing special cameras and instrumentation for capturing light fields in motion such as arrays of video cameras affixed to a globe. Another development was Light Stage 6 where subjects were placed within a sphere with an enormous number of lights that could be selectively lit one at a time to capture an enormous reflective light field that enabled the subject to be lit after the fact either through selection or by being controlled by an HDRI (high dynamic range image) illumination map. For moving subjects, he created an experiment by doing a high-speed recording of a man on a treadmill where every 30th of a second 30 light directions were recorded that could be superimposed upon a single high-speed image frame where the figure was essentially frozen. This recording enabled a live subject to walk through a virtual environment and have their lighting change and adjust as the figure walked from shade to sunlight. This is like the global illumination technique in computer graphics where a 360 image is photographed of a real environment and mapped to a sphere surrounding a computer-graphic character. This photo map becomes the light source that illuminates the figure in a realistic fashion, mimicking the color, bounce, and key light direction as they would have struck a subject in the actual environment. This tremendous amount of oversampled data allows for photo-real reproduction and a wide range of post manipulation, but the processing power required is staggering.

These methods remain expensive and elusive for the independent filmmaker for the time being but may find a home for the specialized VR experiences of today.

Holographic video capture or free viewpoint video

Microsoft developed a technique where the subject is placed in a circular green room where they are flatly lit from all sides with soft LED lights. Dozens of synchronized video cameras record all 360-degree views simultaneously. At the end of the capture, the data (approximately 600 GB per minute) are sent to the computationally heavy rendering process. What comes back is a flatly lit photo-realistic performance capture of an actor in motion that can be placed anywhere in space once isolated from the green background. A cell phone that uses the Apple ARKit will be able to take the phone's camera image and through software analysis determine where ground planes are to enable the operator to place the 3D hologram figure within the scene. The system will also compute this positioning data frame-for-frame, so as you move about the area, the composited 3D figure will "stick" to the ground plane and change in perspective as the camera is moved about. The hologram is completely free from the confines of traditional 2D compositing as the moving figure can be made large or small with the manipulation of fingers upon the touch screen. It is truly remarkable and revolutionary. This is Microsoft's mission statement about the holographic video capture:

> We believe, like a lot of others working in this space, that volumetric computing is the next wave of human computer interaction. AR/VR/MR/XR—all of these are the beginning of freeing humans from being chained to a 2D screen bound by a bezel. That future needs all sorts of content, and demands we create a new grammar of experience building and storytelling. Having *authentic* human content is critical for deeper engagement. Our team's mission is to empower creators to make holographic video accessible for any device—from what's in your pocket now to whatever the next generation of devices become.

Microsoft's mixed reality studios will offer turnkey capture services, consultation, and tool creation for shooting material and post production. The playback of the final rendered capture will be accessible on a wide spectrum of platforms such as tablets, mobile phones, HoloLens, VR, etc. They will also license the technology to others so they can build their own stage. As of the time of writing, two stages are in existence in Los Angeles and London with more to follow.

The figures can also be placed in a virtual setting and observed with virtual reality goggles allowing you to walk around them or dance with them. The possibilities for instructional interaction and entertainment are enormous. For motion picture production it becomes the next phase in the fabulous time slice effect of being able to freeze motion while moving around the scene. In the time slice technique dozens of still cameras had to be aligned on a single path around the subject to simultaneously capture a frozen frame from a number of viewpoints to obtain the effect. No deviation of the camera trajectory could be made without rebuilding the pathway. The holographic video technique allows for infinite flexibility along with the ability to relight the moving figures after the fact. Since the initial capture is flatly lit with no "baked in" directional light these photo map bubbles can be lit in the virtual world with a synthetic key light to introduce modeling and cast real shadows

Figure 9.10 *Four views from a single time stamp render of the 360 holographic scan of myself. The bottom image shows the dense polygon framework beneath the video texture map of my image. The face area has many more polygons assigned to that area to preserve detail. Courtesy of Microsoft Mixed Reality Capture Studios.*

Figure 9.11 *The Apple ARKit software determines the ground plane from the background image for proper placement of the figure in the scene. Note the white polygon plane aligned to the floor on the left. With this data the 3D image can be shrunk and placed upon a different surface such as a table or a chair as on the right as seen in a cell phone. Courtesy of Microsoft Mixed Reality Capture Studios.*

in the environment. The Microsoft system does an amazing job capturing the full figure and even close-ups with amazing detail. There are other systems that are designed to create holographic video of entire stadiums with all cameras lensing from a far distance. Shooting a larger space results in a loss of resolution but good enough to determine the accuracy of a referee's call if the outcome is in question. The company has created an excellent video that breaks down the technical breakthroughs of this amazing technique (https://www.youtube.com/watch?v=SkJG-uFU2yA).

Current limitations of holographic video

Blurring and fine details become a challenge for the technique. Hair is best sprayed down to prevent unwanted frizz or bounce, collars are taped flat to avoid confusing shadows in the render process, and clothing is best left neutral with no patterns and has contrast against the universal green background visible in all the camera views. Objects such as fast-moving golf clubs would tend to disappear entirely, and it is best to have such instruments pantomimed and replaced with a CG element. When the moving capture is observed on playback, one notices a lack of any blur much like the effect of a sharp stop-motion puppet composited against a motion-blurred human in an early Ray Harryhausen film. Of course, that would be in a raw first-generation view of the hologram against real life. In the cinema setting, post processing would address these minor flaws to obtain flawless integration of the video hologram with traditional 2D cinematography. In the near future we will see the technique of holoportation where live-streaming feed of 3D scans can be sent to a distant location where they can be viewed with VR glasses enabling one to see and communicate with a three-dimensional ghost version of the caller on the other end of the line.

Creating a photo-real skydome with still photography

Virtual sets unlike traditional sets can be unlimited in scope and designed so they are a true 360-degree all-immersive environment. The furthermost area in such an environment will be the horizon and sky or skydome. For photo-real renditions one needs to create a photographic panorama to map to the skydome.

The basic idea of creating a 360 panorama involves using a special camera to shoot an environment in all directions as efficiently as possible. The simplest method of doing this is to use two cameras equipped with ultra-wide-angle fisheye lenses where each camera captures 180 degrees or more of a 360 view. The edges of both these images are then "stitched" together to create a seamless cyclorama. One such camera is the Kodak PixPro camera used for capturing 360-degree cinema movies. While each fisheye image is in 4K resolution, one must keep in mind that when used for a virtual backdrop a much smaller portion of the image might be re-imaged by a virtual camera that could result in the background becoming soft due to low resolution (you might be shooting a 720 × 486 extraction off a 4K background image and outputting it to 1920 × 1080). The other issue with the dual fisheye 360 camera is that the sensors of the two cameras are separated as are the lenses leading to parallax

Figure 9.12 *The Kodak PixPro camera with dual fisheye lenses and sensors.*

Figure 9.13 *The unwrapped 360 image that results when both fisheye images from the PixPro are stitched together. Keep in mind that when used for a VR set, only a small portion of the image will be used, which could lead to loss of resolution in the background. It is for this reason that multiple camera 360 systems are often used for high-end VR projects.*

Figure 9.14 *Canon still camera on a nodal mount.*

OFF NODAL
PARALLAX SHIFT WITH PAN

ON NODAL
NO PARALLAX SHIFT WITH PAN

Figure 9.15 *Finding the nodal is a process of trial and error. If the two posts get out of alignment during a pan, adjust the lens position pan, observe, and repeat until the posts do not shift away from each other. When the posts stay the same distance apart during a pan you are on nodal.*

displacement of the imagery such that the stitching will only be seamless at a certain distance from the lens, typically 10–15 feet. If a subject comes closer than that they will begin to tear and separate at the stitching plane. A better approach is to use a larger number of pictures with longer focal-length lenses with a single still camera mounted so that it pans around the nodal point of the lens. If the camera is rotated about the nodal point there will be no perspective shift between objects. If there is enough overlap between the images then the stitch will be truly seamless. In the next section we will examine how to create a seamless panoramic background for use in a virtual environment.

Lens choice and settings

For my panorama I used a Canon Rebel that was capable of shooting 4K and RAW images. Shooting RAW is very important to use as original elements for stitching as there will be a lot more dynamic range in the image. Dynamic range is the ability to resolve a wide range of exposure from dark to light in a smooth gradation. For instance, in an 8-bit jpeg photo you have only 256 steps from black to white. If you created a virtual skydome with this material, you run the risk of creating Mach bands in the sky that appear as zebra stripes where the sky abruptly goes from one shade of blue to another without a smooth transition. This is because the range of values is too small to resolve the gradation of the sky, so the computer does its best to accommodate and creates bands of values through the sky. You can think of this as the computer only having 256 shades of gray instead of the thousand shades it really needs.

Shooting 4K with a longer focal length such as a 24 mm will capture a smaller section of the environment at 4K. After stitching a multitude of narrower view images together, the final resolution of the panorama will be quite large and have more than enough pixels to maintain clarity in the image. When shooting several stills to be stitched it is best to lock the camera on manual settings so there are no auto focus or exposure changes as the camera goes from view to view.

Finding the nodal

One can either purchase a nodal mount or create a mount that allows the camera to slide back and forth from the center of rotation of the tripod allowing the lens to be positioned atop the center at the point where the light rays converge within the lens. The process of finding nodal is empirical. When in the field, you can set the camera pointing at two telephone poles where one is close and the other farther away so that the edges of the poles seem to barely meet. Once you find this composition, pan the camera and look at the gap between the poles. If the poles widen apart or merge together this is an indication that you are not on nodal. Loosen the mount and move the camera and lens closer or further from the center and pan again. You will have arrived at nodal when the gap between the poles does not change during the pan. See Figure 9.15.

Leveling the camera, overlap, and sun compensation

For a smooth stitch, make sure that the camera is level and at a height that prevents foreground objects from being so close that they become out of focus and problematic. In this case I made sure that I was high and far enough away from Sagebrush so that there would not be an issue. Objects that are very close to the camera will need to be true photogrammetry where three-dimensional photo objects need to be created or purchased for inclusion into your scene. Photogrammetry-generated models are available at the Unreal® Marketplace.

As you pan the camera it is important to leave a certain amount of the previous photo in the next view you are taking. For example, if there is a tree at the right-hand side of the frame in picture one, make sure that same tree is seen in the left-hand side of picture two. If your tripod has degree markings, you can make a note of how many degrees it took to arrive at this situation and then merely repeat the degrees until you have shot the full 360 view.

Figure 9.16 *Overlap of images and blocking the sun.*

Figure 9.17 *The steps to create a panorama with a synthetic sky.*

As you get closer to the sun you will have to deal with flare. When the sun is not in the shot but just out of frame you should use your hand or a sunshield on the lens to cut out the flare. When the sun is in the shot, feel free to place your finger in front of the sun to block the flare. Later on, in post, you will remove your hand and create a synthetic sky.

Stitching the images

Once you have assembled the collection of images, you can load them into a stitching software such as Mistika VR or Kolor Autopano Giga and allow the computer to do the dirty work. Usually the stitch comes out fine but in some cases, like this example at the top of Figure 9.17, we see that while the terrain stitched flawlessly, we now have dark bands in the sky area. This is the result of our 24 mm lens having some subtle vignette shadowing around the edges. This slight darkening of the peripheral is barely noticeable on a single image but after stitching, the darkened edges join and make the effect pronounced.

One way to solve the banding issue is to take the file into Photoshop® and create a mask based on the tones of the image. In this case I converted the image to black-and-white and adjusted the levels to make the sky bright white and darken the horizon elements to create a demarcation. The soft mask of the horizon made up of trees and foliage was extended by manual masking to create a mask that only reveals the color ground plane. A synthetic sky was then created using the gradation tool and tones from the actual sky to create a smooth unblemished sky with no banding. Noise was added to the sky to help it blend with the stitched photography below. Since the entire sky was now synthetic, the real sun that was blotted out was merely used as reference for the creation of a synthetic sun with halo that was blended atop the sky.

Final touches

To create a useable ground plane for our performers I decided to shoot down on some decking from the second floor and correct for perspective in Photoshop®. I shot this in shade to obtain an ambient-lit photo element that could respond to virtual light without having shadows "baked in" as they are in the stitched panorama. In other words, when the subject stands on the green floor with a hard shadow cast upon it, the deck photograph will illuminate in the same way as the floor so the deck will be lit with the key and shadows will hold true when this image is texture mapped to a polygon plane within the Unreal® environment. An alternative to making a sky in Photoshop® is to use the default skydome in the game engine and place it beyond the stitched photo landscape.

Figure 9.18 *Deck in fill light only.*

Figure 9.19 *The color- and perspective-corrected deck is mapped to a polygon plane suspended in the middle of the photo cyclorama. When the green-screen live performer is composited into the set, he or she will cast a believable shadow on the deck and can be lit to match the baked-in lighting of the panoramic background.*

For a background with moving imagery you would need to shoot with a high resolution 360 multi-video camera rig, but if you are on a budget a simple Canon camera can do wonders just using still imagery. In the next chapter we will continue our exploration of creating the virtual studio with limited resources.

Chapter 10
So, you don't have a million dollars

Many schools are budget challenged and extremely cautious about investments in technology that becomes obsolete so quickly. As an instructor and visual effects supervisor working on small independent films I have learned to improvise and make do while still achieving both educational and production goals with a minimum of compromise. These methods address the need for directors and filmmakers to be exposed to the post processes without having to deeply dive into the software. I have seen first-hand the frustration of filmmakers when exposed to computer graphic software for the first time. They are absolutely overwhelmed and disheartened. It would be like saying you can't drive a car without being a licensed engine mechanic. Forcing above-the-line creatives into the high-level CG discipline will do nothing more than dissuade them from using and furthering the art. Filmmakers want to find sets and shoot their ideas in them. They don't want to build CG sets or know all the technical details. To address this situation, I propose using the less complex Adobe® Photoshop® and Adobe® After Effects® software tools in order to make the digital backlot process more accessible for the beginner whose work as a filmmaker will only improve as they now understand the concepts and can (after their experience) communicate and rely on digital artists to execute their ideas using more sophisticated game engine tools. This chapter will focus on achieving the digital backlot technique with simple bare bones tool sets.

163

360 camera effects

Elementary explorations into 360 cinema can be done with inexpensive cameras such as the Kodak PixPro mentioned in Chapter 9 on photogrammetry. The great thing about these cameras is that they work best by being locked down in one spot as the viewer is expected to explore the scene by either changing the view of the cell phone playing back the shot, using virtual goggles, or using a mouse to change the point of view when viewing on YouTube. Once the images are stitched together, they become a fixed camera element where any number of clever composites can be executed.

As an example, an interview can be done using the PixPro with lights and sound technicians in full view. After the interview the lights and personnel are removed and a "clean plate" is shot from the same position to provide another element to erase the lights and crew. When the stitched elements are brought into After Effects® it is a simple matter to erase objects, put in green-screen characters, composite clouds outside of rotoscoped windows, and add animation or any number of tricks as the unwrapped image becomes a simple 2D

Figure 10.1 *In an unwrapped 360 cinema image, a sky replacement becomes a snap. No match moving required. For a seamless sky replacement stitch, it is best to match the pixel patterns on either end at the stitch line.*

image that requires no match moving or tracking. Once the effect is done the final render is simply uploaded to YouTube for 3D viewing.

Do post moves instead of camera tracking

The easiest way for a student to achieve an inexpensive digital backlot is to eliminate live camera tracking all together. The best way to achieve this is to lock off all the camera angles and shoot the shots at high resolution with the intention of cropping in and moving within the frame. An example would be to shoot the shots at 4K with the final resolution being high-definition (Hi-Def) or 1920 × 1080. Using this combination there will be no resolution loss and plenty of flexibility to do camera moves in post. If the locked-off green-screen composite is rendered as a 4K movie then the composite can be reloaded into After Effects® to execute a pan and scan move rendered at Hi-Def without the need for a virtual camera. If moves are done on a 2D image in this manner then the compromise will be no perspective shift and the shots will look like pan and scan moves on a flat image. If, however, the layers used such as green-screen foreground (FG) and multi-layer set elements are made 3D then dimensional perspective moves can easily be obtained using a virtual camera in After Effects and like the Reality™ system the composited live action can be placed within the set and behind objects.

Use real photo backgrounds instead of computer graphic sets

To avoid the large learning curve of computer graphics students can be introduced to CG backgrounds by texture mapping photography onto simple

Figure 10.2 *This miniature was shot at 4K resolution. As you can see by the Hi-Def extraction, we have plenty of room to zoom in, pan, and tilt without loss of resolution in the final delivery.*

Figure 10.3 *Laying a mirror flat against the plane you are shooting allows you to quickly align your camera to be straight on to the subject. Position the camera so that the reflection of the lens is centered on the center mark of the camera's eyepiece. Remove the mirror and take the shot.*

polygon planes generated in After Effects®. This also has the advantage of introducing students to the discipline of photogrammetry. The biggest challenge when shooting live sets is being flat on to the building's surface and to shoot in ambient shadowless light. We want ambient light to enable virtual lights to light our set. The easiest way to conduct this exercise is by using miniatures such as doll houses under controlled conditions. To shoot a wall flat on, the fastest and easiest way is to place a mirror on the wall and position the camera so that the lens of the camera is seen in the mirror reflected in the dead center of the eyepiece.

Scale and pixels

In computer graphics that involve tracking, all the virtual sets are made to be full size so that a meter is a meter. This is so that as the live-action camera moves, its counterpart moves the same distance. Since we are not doing live tracking but post moves there is no need to create accurate full-size models so we can create synthetic backgrounds to an arbitrary scale. In the case of shooting photographs to create flat-sided three-dimensional models, it is important to relate actual measurements to pixels. As an example, if you were to recreate a 10 × 15-foot room with 8-foot-high walls you could decide that 100 pixels equal 1 foot and in Photoshop® create new layers that represent the room dimensions with each layer being a separate wall on top of a larger canvas. The 10 × 8-foot wall becomes 100 × 800 pixels. Now if at some point the film frame will be filled by that wall and your final resolution is 1920 × 1080, then

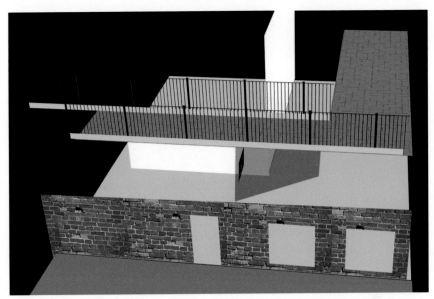

Figure 10.4 *In this example I went to an art gallery and measured out the actual dimensions of the floor plan and upper walkway and created layers in Photoshop® using a scale of 100 pixels per foot. Once all the elements were made and connected, an accurate simple layout of the gallery space was achieved. The brick wall was a photo texture added on top of one of the planes with portions deleted to create a door and windows.*

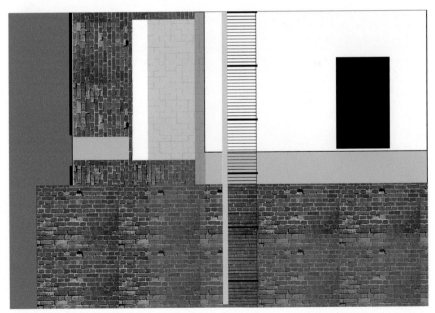

Figure 10.5 *This flattened image shows all the separate wall layers stacked atop of each other on top of the large bottom layer. This view of the layers is before they are turned into 3D layers and repositioned to create the 3D gallery above.*

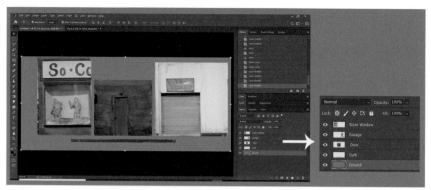

Figure 10.6 *This shows the images of the miniature I shot laid out as layers in Photoshop®. The size of the gray ground plane is 3452 × 2208 pixels, which demonstrates that these elements have plenty of resolution to create a 3D model in After Effects® for a 1920 × 1080 final shot. This is saved as a Photoshop® document and ported into After Effects® as a composition. Adobe® product screenshot(s) reprinted with permission from Adobe®.*

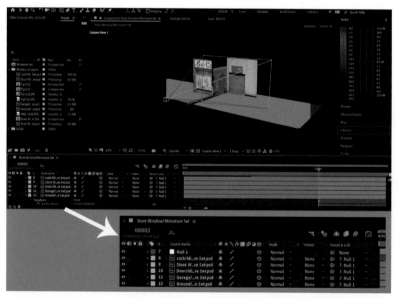

Figure 10.7 *The close-up view of the layers showing how each layer becomes a three-dimensional set piece that is able to move in the X, Y, and Z axes once the cube icon is activated. Once the layers are positioned so that they form the walls of the set they are "parented" to a null object shown on the far right so that the transform controls in the "Null 1" layer will move all the set pieces together as one.*

you would want the dimension to be multiplied by 200 pixels per foot, making the layer 2000 × 1600. A photo of a brick wall that is at least that large could be inserted as another layer and merged with the wall layer to add it as a texture map creating a brick wall that can be imported into After Effects®.

Figure 10.8 *The Photoshop® layers after positioning in 3D to create the set.*

Figure 10.9 *Adding a point light layer and making sure all the layers accept light and cast shadows in the materials section of the layer controls.*

Shooting the live action

As in the game engine example we can create a camera in After Effects® and find the angle and do a screen grab to make a storyboard. Unlike the high-end system that automatically links the real and virtual cameras, the After Effects® technique will need to create a virtual camera that matches the camera that you

Figure 10.10 *Adding an ambient light layer for the final touches. This general lighting can be adjusted afterward to better match the live-action lighting. Note how the ground planes have no texture map and take on a plastic appearance.*

Figure 10.11 *Using a header is a great way to expand the screen when you don't have enough height. It covers the actress's head when she is in the foreground yet is high enough to let her pass under to get in the final position for the screen. It only needs to cover the action. In this case the hanging card header is a sheet of green poster board obtained from the local dollar store. The orange area shows the rotoscoped mask to place the figure and floor within the set.*

shot the live action with and then adjust the CG background until it matches the perspective and places the ground of the virtual set under the feet of the live performer. For shooting the live action we can either use a real floor for the subject to stand on that will replace the virtual floor we created, or we can pull a shadow off green. It is easier and better to shoot the subject standing on a real floor with real shadows but for this case study I will illustrate both. This case is a challenging example of dramatic high-contrast film noir lighting.

The best method for isolating the figure in order to create a photo-real virtual paper doll cut-out that can be placed within the 3D set that allows for dimensional moves is to shoot the figure standing on a mirrored floor to eliminate spill and bounce, and provide a cleanly lit floor area. The reflection is removed with rotoscoping.

Figure 10.12 *Here is the final composite with the actress standing on her real floor to obtain superior lighting and shadow interaction for a high-contrast film noir effect. Keep in mind that if you decide to use a real floor you will only be able to do two-dimensional moves with no perspective change (pan and tilt only). A 3D move such as a push in will instantly misalign the real floor with the virtual background.*

Figure 10.13 *Here is a composite where the actress stood on a green floor. Without the clean plate process, it is very difficult to pull shadows off a green floor that aren't "buzzy." This shadow was softened with the Keylight software's de-spot black control that essentially softens the noise.*

Figure 10.14 *Another technique that works well is to take a clean cut-out of an actor against a green screen without a shadow and use that as a paper doll cut-out that can cast a shadow but not accept light. This works well within a wide range of lighting angles but would fail in the previous example of Figure 10.13 as the light was directly to the side and our paper doll cut-out woman would amount to a mere slit of a shadow at best.*

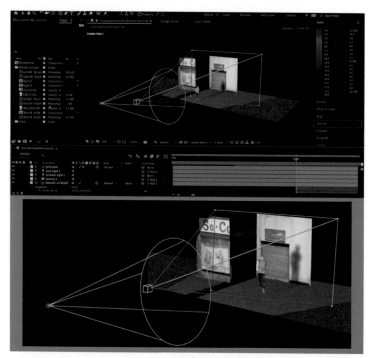

Figure 10.15 *This custom view in After Effects® displays the paper doll technique. The box projecting the rectangular view represents the virtual camera shooting the dimensional layers where the green-screen man is on a transparent plane in front of the set. The small circular origin at the far left is the spot light that shines upon the figure but does not light up the figure (as that layer was told not to accept light), however it does use the cut-out to create and cast a shadow on the wall (as that layer was told to cast shadows and the ground and garage background were told to accept shadows). It is a very strange universe indeed. Adobe® product screenshot(s) reprinted with permission from Adobe®.*

Figure 10.16 *If the camera moves in space, one can achieve a fully dimensional move. The difficulty arises when actors move toward and away from camera. Since the actor's image is on a fixed plane the image doesn't move in space but merely gets larger or smaller. To compensate, the plane the image is on must animate its size and position to place the performer properly in the space. If the actor walked forward 5 feet then the transparent plane the actor's image is on would also move forward 5 feet and reduce in size so that the enlargement of the figure would be correct as if the actor walked forward in the 3D set. The key to avoiding this workflow is to limit the actor's movements to be only side-to-side.*

The problem of Z-axis moves with the performer moving forward or back

Since the green–screen camera is locked off you will note that as the performer walks away from the camera their image will become smaller. If this paper doll cut-out is put in the virtual space in a fixed spot the paper doll image will become smaller as well, which may cause the connection between the ground plane and the feet to change. If the virtual camera moves forward the set may increase in size differently than the paper doll figure that will increase in size at the same time as its image is shrinking. For Z-axis moves toward and away from the camera, post animation compensation will need to be done to correct these issues. If the performers stay in one plane along the horizontal axis during their performance and don't walk forward and back, there will be no problem with Z-axis camera moves as their image will always stay the same size in the same plane in the 3D set.

Matching the virtual camera to the live-action camera

As with the earliest visual-effects techniques, it is important that the same camera and lens is used for both the foreground and background elements. In traditional work it was a simple matter to just use the same camera and lens for both elements. In this case we must create a virtual camera to match our real camera. To start with, make a note of the camera you are shooting with such as a Canon 5D Mark IV and the focal length of the lens you are shooting with such as 20 mm. Lock off the camera and shoot a shot of your live action against a green screen. Once you have this shot go to an online calculator such as this one from Abel Cine to quickly discover the sensor size of your camera (https://www.abelcine.com/articles/blog-and-knowledge/tools-charts-and-downloads/abelcine-fov-tool-20).

In this case we find that the sensor size is 36 × 24.

In After Effects® you can import the shot of the actor against the green screen into the timeline and then create a camera layer. When the camera settings box comes up we can use our knowledge of the Canon sensor size and lens to create a matching virtual camera.

The camera type should be a one-node camera, which means that when you move the camera body by panning, tilting, or pushing in, the view will change just like a regular camera. A two-node camera can move the camera in this way and also by adjusting what the lens is looking at, which can be a bit confusing. It is easier to keep it as a one-node type.

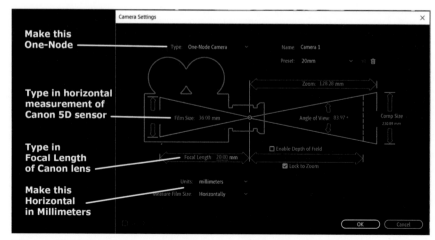

Figure 10.17 *Using the camera settings box. Adobe® product screenshot(s) reprinted with permission from Adobe®.*

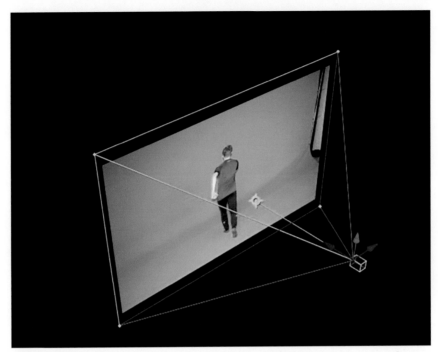

Figure 10.18 *Positioning the virtual camera to match the original camera. Adobe®
product screenshot(s) reprinted with permission from Adobe®.*

The type of units and their direction is important for matching, in this case
the Canon camera sensor is measured horizontally in millimeters so you put
in the same methods of measurement for the virtual tool set and type in the
36 mm sensor size and the 20 mm focal length (to match a film camera, you
would need to change the units of measurement to inches. An Academy
aperture for example is 0.868 inches. The focal length will always be in
millimeters).

When the camera is created you will have a matching camera that will need to
be positioned to match the location of the Canon camera.

To get an approximate starter distance, adjust the virtual camera to shoot the
3D green-screen layer image until its view matches the original shot (the edges
of the virtual camera frame meet the edges of the green-screen image frame).
This will place the subject (which now becomes like a paper doll cut-out) in a
good position in space relative to the camera. Use a keyer to remove the green
screen, making that portion of the layer transparent and import your virtual set.
You can now position your virtual set (connecting all the layers together using
a null object) to fit with the live-action subject such as making the floor meet
the feet as shown in Figure 10.14.

Using this starting position, you can then freely move the virtual camera by panning and tilting, and slight moves in and out, and up and down. You will not be able to circle around the figure as the subject is just a flat cut-out and will not change dimensionally. In the Zero Density system even though the image is also a flat cut-out, its shape and content (front to profile view) will change as the camera circles about to create the illusion of a dimensional figure.

One way to get an inexpensive opportunity to utilize a portion of the Zero Density system is to obtain their Reality Keyer™ plug-in for After Effects®. If the student locks off the camera and shoots both a clean plate (the green screen without the subject) and a take of the performer against the green screen, the keyer will pull an excellent quality composite complete with naturalistic shadows just like the high-end system.

For students who want to generate virtual sets using Unreal®, the software is free to download, and inexpensive sets can be purchased. Screen grabs or renders of the environment can be loaded into After Effects® to complete the composite.

For schools that have some resources

If the school has a modest budget, I would recommend using the Unreal® software, which is free and purchasing a Mo-Sys tracking system with the Unreal® plug-in. Mo-Sys StarTracker can be used with older cameras so really the only new item to be acquired is the StarTracker. The system has a chroma keyer to enable the students to do composites within the virtual sets in real time. For higher quality I would suggest recording the raw background and the raw green screen-footage separately and compositing later using Keylight or other blue/green compositing software in After Effects®.

For motion capture I would suggest an inertial suit such as a Nansense or Synertial. It will be less precise than the more expensive optical system and will need to be away from metal and Wi-Fi interference but should be fine for the educational setting. I would forgo the facial motion capture and make use of post animation for dialog scenes. This process will take longer but will be a good learning experience as even facial motion capture needs fine tuning in post to be perfect.

For schools that have even more resources

Another system that allows you to insert live action within synthetic sets is Pixotope™ Director (https://www.futureuniverse.com/product).

This is like the Reality™ system, but with a simpler user interface. It has its own keying technology but can also accept other keyers such as the magnificent Blackmagic Ultimatte keyer (https://www.blackmagicdesign.com/products/ultimatte).

I highly recommend the Ultimatte keyer as the system's lineage goes all the way back to its inventor, Petro Vlahos, mentioned in Chapter 1. It continues to be the preferred keyer for many high-end productions.

For film schools that have more of a filmmaking focus I would suggest the turnkey Halide Effects system from Lightcraft, highlighted in Chapter 4 (https://halidefx.com).

For schools with devoted curriculum for the discipline

For schools with a focus on the study of Unreal® Game Engine software and asset creation, I would suggest the Reality™ system highlighted in Chapter 5 (https://www.zerodensity.tv).

Students devoted to the study of Unreal® would benefit from learning this system as an excellent complement to Unreal® and would serve to make the student even more marketable after graduation. Any number of cameras and camera-tracking systems are accepted into the system and it has ready-made templates to accommodate a variety of virtual-studio scenarios such as VR or augmented reality (AR). The node-based architecture allows for extreme flexibility and fine tuning of student projects. Keep in mind that the system is powerful and sophisticated and will need dedicated personal to keep it humming. In my opinion it would not be for schools that don't have the resources or IT to trouble shoot and correct the inevitable rewiring or software entanglements that eager students tend to generate in their creative journeys. I have heard of situations where schools purchase sophisticated systems that wind up sitting idle because they did not think to staff a tech person dedicated to the running and operation of complex systems.

For motion capture I recommend the Qualysis system highlighted in Chapter 3 that has its own resolver so there is no need for additional software such as motion builder (https://www.qualisys.com).

It is an excellent high-resolution system that, when used along with facial capture technology such as Faceware (https://www.facewaretech.com), will allow the student to experience and execute state-of-the-art technology to prepare them for the high-tech workforce of virtual entertainment.

In the ever-changing current of technological advancement it is futile to attempt to set anything in stone and say this is the tool to use. The companies and technologies I have highlighted win my respect for their longevity and history of use in the production landscape.

In the next chapter we will do a case study of an entire set-up involving the game engine, 3D compositing, and performance capture.

Chapter 11

Production case studies

What follows will be a blow-by-blow description of a production shoot in a virtual studio.

Case study 1
Planning begins

The shoot involves a live-action dancer in a computer-generated dance hall who interacts with a computer-graphic cartoon character who is mute. The live performer suggests a dance, the music plays, and they both dance together to see who has the best moves.

First, questions begin with what is needed for delivery.

1. Format: Apple Pro Res 4:2:2 HQ 1920 × 1080 59.94 i.
2. Number of cameras: Two: one locked off and one moving.
3. Sound: Yes, but only for live performer as the character is mute.
4. Mocap: Yes, mute performer with simple hands (no finger capture). This determined that the Qualysis optical system would be the best tool with no need for inertial or facial capture.

Virtual set analysis

The virtual dance hall set that was chosen is explored for stage area and lighting. One potential issue was lighting produced by rotating red, green and blue lights within one region of the set. To match this exotic lighting would be very problematic using practical lights along with the synchronization problem of having a red light hit the subject while the virtual red light hit the set. The other issue with this lighting if reproduced on the real green stage is the effect upon keying. If a pure green light were to hit the subject, they would essentially begin to disappear since they would become green also. The solution is to not light the subject with exotic lights but let them remain steadily lit with white light and record the raw green screen and the raw background (BG) separately for post compositing. The live composite would serve as a previz element for editorial and be replaced with the post composites later. The post composite would enable the ability to animate color-correction controls to tone the performer with the required red, green, and blue tints to synchronize with the background lighting. In this case the production company chose not to complicate matters and removed the exotic light effect.

Equipment needs

Both cameras were tuned in and available in house (Blackmagic Design BMD–CINEURSA4K and Blackmagic Design EF URSA EF 4K), but we needed to have six recorders based on each camera needing to record:

1. Live composite Camera A.
2. Live composite Camera B.
3. Raw green element Camera A.
4. Raw green element Camera B.
5. BG only for Camera A.
6. BG only for Camera B.

Additional hard-drive recorders were rented for the shoot.

Main computer

For this production a custom-built CUBIX system was used to best accommodate the needs of both the Unreal® Game Engine and the Reality™ software according to their specifications and beyond. The all-important video card was a Quadro P6000 though other systems such as Pixotope™ Director can play well with an RTX 2080 video card. The bottom line is that it is cheaper to custom build the computer hardware than to buy an off-the-shelf ready-built system if you have the technical talent available to do the build.

Figure 11.1 *The video capture tools featured here are an ATEM production studio 4K switcher, a smart video hub 20 × 20 router, and several 12G SDI Hyperdeck recorders all from Blackmagic Design. Courtesy of Mobile Motion MoCap.*

Stage and equipment set-up

In order to accomplish the effect of a motion-capture puppet interacting with a live actor against a green screen with both composited in real time within a virtual set, the stage needed to be divided into two areas so that the mocap performer would be off-camera and separate from the live performer. This separation eliminates a great deal of post work that would be required to eliminate the image of the mocap actor if they appeared in the live-action footage. Monitors are placed so that both the live actor and the mocap actor could see the final composite and be able to adjust their performances so that the virtual and the live would interact properly. In order to keep good eyelines, the monitors might be placed where the other actor would be. In this case it was easier to place the monitor for the mocap performer's eyeline, but the live actor had most of their performance facing the camera and would need to turn to the side looking within the green-screen stage and imagine where the virtual character would be. Since there was dancing involved having the live actor see the composite in a monitor placed next to the camera would allow them to dance and not accidentally run into the space the virtual actor was dancing in.

The mocap stage

This area was closer to the camera and to the side. As the field of view of the live-action lens spreads out from the camera to the stage it became relatively easy to have the mocap actor perform and still be outside the view of the taking camera. The mocap performance space was taped off for best capture area along with the all-important zero point. Qualysis cameras were positioned high on the grid so as not to be seen by the live-action camera. There were also multiple mocap cameras on large portable tripods to help view the mocap space. Once the stage was set the "wand dance" was done to insure a good performance volume. At the time of writing, in order to create a live mocap performance, the pipeline is Qualysis to Motion Builder to Live Link to provide bridge communication. Qualysis provides the motion data and the motion builder attaches this data to the skeleton of the character, which is then imported into the game engine set.

The live-action stage

A zero point was created for the camera where the camera could see the entire green-screen cove and the widest zoom setting. This position was important to be able to take a picture of the entire green stage in order to map it into the virtual cyclorama within the compositing system. Measurements were taken of the height, width, and depth of the green area along with the radius of the curves that connect the walls and floor. Another measurement is made from the camera's zero point to the back wall, and from the zero point to one of the inside corners of the green-screen cove. This is in order to locate the virtual green cove at the proper distance from the virtual camera to match their real counterparts.

Figure 11.2 *The mocap staging area is downstage and to the left of the green-screen stage area. The Qualysis cameras surround this area to observe the mocap performer. Courtesy of Mobile Motion MoCap.*

ZERO POINT→

Figure 11.3 *The wand dance is used to create the capture volume. Note the zero-point L bracket on the floor. Courtesy of Mobile Motion MoCap.*

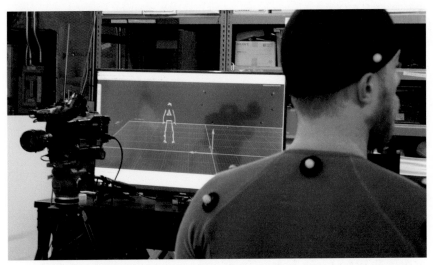

Figure 11.4 *The monitor is placed to one side of the taking camera for both the live action and the mocap performer to observe the CG figure and the performance interaction. This monitor shows the skeletal view but will be switched to the composite view for the takes. Courtesy of Mobile Motion MoCap.*

Figure 11.5 *Measuring to obtain the location of the virtual cyclorama. All measurements are metric and will be unique for each stage situation. Courtesy of Mobile Motion MoCap.*

Tracking

After the retroreflective markers are attached to the ceiling, the Mo-Sys tracking camera set-up is executed as described in Chapter 4 on camera tracking. The proper cable hooks-ups are connected and tests for tracking are made. See Figure 4.10.

Live-action camera set-up

Lenses are checked for focus and, if using a video camera, back focus is also adjusted to make sure that the focus holds true throughout the zoom range. We also make sure that signals from both cameras and the tracking system are in sync. In order to synchronize video and computer signals, a generator locking device (Gen lock) is used as a reference input signal that other devices are slave to. In this case the cameras were running at 1920 × 1080 59.94 interlace. Exposure is adjusted after the lighting set-up is finished.

Figure 11.6 *The retroreflective targets on the pipes and ceiling. Larger markers are used for the higher areas. The more markers the better. Courtesy of Mobile Motion MoCap.*

Lighting prep

We review the equipment needed and make sure there are spare instruments and bulbs available if needed. Only one half of the green stage needs to be lit. For beauty lighting we will use soft key, soft fill, and hard kicker. When hanging lights, it is always a good idea to attach any tools to belts or wrist bracelets to prevent them being accidentally dropped. The same is true for mounting lights on high pipes. Always use an auxiliary wire safety lanyard in case the main clamp gives way for some reason. Since foot traffic and ladders will be on the floor of the green area, Ram Board® is placed on top of the green floor to protect it as the lighting instruments are hung and directed.

- 5K Tungsten Fresnel lamps are hung from the back of the stage with single scrims and diffusion to dim down the brightness. The barn doors are positioned to cut the light from hitting the floor and shining into the camera lens. The only area that these instruments light will be the actor's hair and shoulders. Always be sure to wear gloves when adjusting these types of lights as they get extremely hot.
- The rest of the lights are Cine Light 120 LED panels that are set to 3200 Kelvin color temperature to match the Tungsten kicker lights. These soft lights are arranged to evenly illuminate the walls and floor of the green-screen area. There are extra soft lights placed to one side to create a soft key for modeling of the subject.

If you see something say something

I noticed that as the set was being developed it became a dance studio with a large mirror. While the Reality™ system can indeed create reflections on

Figure 11.7 *The lighting set-up. Note the Ram Board® on top of the green floor as protection to enable ladders and people to set up the lights. To the right we see a monitor on a rolling stand to enable our mocap actor to perform to the composite. The live actors on green will observe the monitor next to the camera. Courtesy of Mobile Motion MoCap.*

floors and walls in front of the subject, a mirror prop is problematic as the mirror reflects another viewpoint. As an example, if a mirror is behind the subject as they face the camera it will reflect the back of the subject. In the case of a virtual mirror there is no second camera taking an image of the back of the subject to use as a reflection. After a brief discussion the mirror was quickly eliminated from the set.

The client visit

About a week before the one-day shoot the main production personnel from the client paid a visit to ascertain how the set-up of the technology was coming along, and to make last-minute creative changes. At this point the mocap was working as well as the green-screen composite to give the client a preview of what they will be working with on the shoot day. The effect is shown on a large monitor and the clients were adjusting the size of the CG puppet compared to an actor, all the while taking cell phone pictures of various options to send to the director. A production meeting was held to firm up last-minute requirements.

1. Format now includes 9 × 16 as well as 16 × 9. This is initially puzzling because one can think of it as a mistaken transposition but in fact it is

to accommodate social media distribution that on some platforms only exists in a frame that is taller than it is wide. This will be accomplished by extracting the 9×16 frame from within the 16×9 video.

2. Need teleprompter for talent.
3. Voice-over (VO) artist will be attending as well and will need to have a microphone.
4. Lavalier microphone and back-up boom microphone needed for performer.
5. Need monitors for two off-stage rooms.
6. Need two monitors for the stage: one for talent and one for production crew.
7. Parking for 22 cars: 31 people expected.
8. Wardrobe rack with steamer plus distilled water.
9. Chairs, tables, ice chests, and catered food.
10. Finalize character and shape of hands, mittens, or three fingers and a thumb.

Sound considerations

The performer will need to be recorded for voice but also needs to hear music to dance. The playback of the music will be lowered during dialog spoken during the dance to provide separation. One can use a separate synced music track to enhance its volume in editing. If an issue occurs with sound, one can always loop the dialog later to eliminate any problems.

Take your shoes off and stay a while

During the relentless running around during set-up and production, one must remember to keep the green-screen floor as unblemished as possible. Before walking on the floor put fabric booties over your shoes or simply take off your shoes and walk on the green floor in your stockings.

The shoot day

The set-up crew arrives a couple of hours before the client's call time to ensure that all the technology is running smoothly, and everything is calibrated. Breakfast and coffee are prepared, and chairs and viewing areas are set. As the clients walk in, dry runs are executed to prepare the director and clients for the proper shooting procedure. The location of the projection cube is adjusted to allow for the compositing of the live action in the proper place within the virtual set. During this stage there will be checks for costume choice against the green screen and last-minute lighting adjustments. In this case, when the actual performer stood on the mark the client felt that more fill lighting needed

Figure 11.8 *The final set-up. The mocap performer strikes a T pose at the head of the shot, the sound is recorded using a boom and the live-action actor stands in the green-screen area where the virtual background and CG character will be composited in real time. Courtesy of Mobile Motion MoCap.*

to be added from below. To accommodate the request the studio was prepared with extra lights, diffusion, reflectors, and power to provide the extra fill in a heartbeat. After the lighting is approved, the green-screen stage is cleared and a new clean plate is created, and the keyer is adjusted again. A new clean plate will need to be taken any time an adjustment is made in the lighting. After the keyer is tuned in, we are ready to shoot. Unlike traditional movie production, there are a few more things to consider when slating that will be added to the call-out checklist of all the stations before the director calls action.

Call outs

Traditional call outs:

1. "Roll Sound" … reply: "Rolling"
2. "Roll Camera" … reply: "Speed"
3. "Marker" … reply: "Scene 7, take 1 marker" (the clapper drops to a click)
4. Director says "Action!"

Virtual call outs:

1. "Roll Sound" … reply: "Rolling"
2. "Roll Camera" … reply: "Speed" (this would be the six recording decks activated as the cameras are always on)

3. "Mocap" ... reply: "Recording" (records mocap data)
4. "VP (virtual production)" ... reply: "Recording" (records camera track information in the game engine)
5. "Marker" ... reply: "Scene 7, take 1 marker"
6. "T pose" ... reply: "Ready" (the T pose is the mocap position starting point)
7. Director says "Action!"

At the end of the take:

1. "Cut"
2. "T pose" ... (the mocap performer strikes the tail T pose again and once recorded the mocap team stops recording)

Depending on the situation or desires of the production team, the call-outs will be modified to conform to the needs of the project.

The production then continues as a traditional production with shooting takes, making camera moves, playing back takes to check quality and performance, and so on until the shoot is completed. With a stable tech stage that has its own cameras, green-screen lights, mocap, computers, and pipeline established, one only need be concerned about special lighting and sound rental for the performer along with other typical production considerations such as makeup, costume, etc.

Figure 11.9 *The final composite.*

Case study 2: When technology goes bad

The previous example is from a production scenario utilizing a well-oiled virtual studio with stable technology. The producer must keep in mind that to have a good working studio it will take at least two solid months to work out the technology and pipelines in order to have a repeatable stable system that will respond as efficiently as the gear in a traditional movie shoot. A virtual set needs at least a month to customize and rig for the production as well. The fictional scenario below is a compilation of an assortment of challenges that come up when the timeline is too short, the software needs work-arounds because a plug-in isn't ready yet, or mysterious video communication issues arise.

Scenario

The producer wants to use his favorite camera from 1989 because he likes the lens and he must shoot in four days.

Day one

The camera is brought in and it is discovered it will not take a Gen lock signal or the Gen lock generator that was provided does not work. Video engineers are called in to analyze the problem. Gen lock cables are switched, the Gen lock generator is checked but the camera does not play well with the newer tech. If the Gen lock cannot be connected the camera-tracking system will not work. An engineer with the tracking system is contacted in Eastern Europe to examine the problem in LA. A system called TeamViewer is used so that the engineer can log in and manipulate the software from across the globe. The entire day is spent going back and forth to try to figure out a Gen lock solution. The engineer looks up the original specs for the old camera and discovers that the camera itself can generate a Gen lock signal through the composite signal and devises a way to connect the monitor output on the camera to the Gen lock in to have the camera be the source of the Gen lock. This issue takes all day to solve.

Two minutes to midnight

No that wasn't the doomsday clock but merely the time in Europe that the engineer attending to our problem stayed up until to create work-arounds to hardware issues and updated software changes. With a tight production schedule, it might very well become a doomsday clock.

Day two

The camera seems to track but the video image is now jittery and halting. The signal goes out at 59.9 frames per second, but the recorded file indicates it is running at 23.9 frames per second. Another call is placed to another engineer in France to sort out the compositing and media–input software. TeamViewer is activated again, and another engineer is kept up until 2:00 in the morning and suggests we must wait until another company opens in the morning in Sweden to address the jittery issue.

Day three

The Swedish engineer comes on board and suggests we need to install a new video card and reload drivers. One of the team runs out to buy a new card and installs it in the computer. This has fixed the jitter, but the tracking is poor. The engineer suggests we take new measurements of the sensor displacement. New measurements are taken, and the engineer adds them to the software, but the tracking still shows sliding of the performer on the ground as the camera is moved. Different numbers are put in the software as the camera is moved to empirically find a tracking setting that works. This takes hours. Things are getting close and then the Internet goes down. It seems that all the systems have unique IP addresses to work with one another, and the Internet allows them to see each other. With the Internet down, the game engine doesn't start. The Internet provider is called in to do an emergency ping to restart the Internet and the connections.

Shoot day

The system is sorta, kinda holding together on a wing and a prayer. The shoot is moving along and then it is discovered that the tracking data is not recording because the data rate is too low. Fortunately, all the raw camera data is being

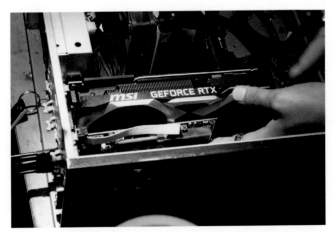

Figure 11.10 *You don't want to be in the position of installing an untested video card at the last minute during a shoot. Courtesy of Mobile Motion MoCap.*

recorded. Since all has failed except for the camera image and the background image, these elements will have to be composited in post production. Since the tracking data is missing, both the live-action footage and the background image will need to be stabilized so that new post moves can be generated during compositing. With all the high tech at hand, the project had to resort to old-school solutions at the end of the day. Due to haste and an insistence on using an outmoded camera the project will need to be completed using a tremendous amount of fix–it time in post.

Conclusion

We are in the pioneering days of this high technology becoming accessible to the independent filmmaker and as such we should not ignore the fact that it is "high" technology with a lot of moving interdependent parts that will require well-trained technicians to operate. Particularly for the game engine and motion capture software. Wonderful films can be created with these amazing tools, but they are not necessarily bullet proof or plug and play like an app on your cell phone. However, if you plan well and provide enough time in pre-production to build, test, and create a smooth pipeline, you too can make your own "Sin City" or "Sherlock Holmes" period piece on an affordable budget.

As we move forward on this one-way ticket to the future, we must keep in mind that the future is in our hands and we determine our own destiny as best we can. To get by we must take a vow to be adaptive but not necessarily adoptive of everything that comes down the pike. As an exciting and rewarding change of pace, Alfonso Cuaron the director of the super high-tech 90% CGI movie *Gravity* (2013) decided to direct another film *Roma* (2018) in black-and-white and used traditional filmmaking methods. Ultimately it is always about the story and the story will inform the method used to tell it. The important thing for the artist is to create, and create what you want, and "how" you want. If artificial intelligence (AI) helps you then use it. If you distrust it and want to say with confidence "I made this," then truly make it your own. Even those with modest means will be able to create fantastic stories depicting their world through their eyes whose vision has been denied from the rest of us either through technical challenges or because of the lack of financing. The important thing is that the ultimate salvation of our humanity will be the ability to communicate and provide a deeper understanding of all sides of this universal adventure called life. This is now more possible than ever before with the technology at hand, be it through virtual backlot moviemaking, traditional filmmaking, or the powerful VR experiences of the future. So, carry on storytellers and light the way.

Chapter 12
Virtual reality
Indistinguishable from magic

This chapter examines the 21st-century phenomenon that is manipulated reality experiences. We look at a brief history of VR/AR/MR (see definitions below) and explore how manipulated reality technology is disrupting storytelling and entertainment as we know it. We scrutinize how this medium is dependent on all of the past technologies covered yet is radically different from everything that preceded it. We end the chapter with a look into the future of VR/AR/MR and what issues await us going forward to the middle of the century. Could this be the Brave New World foretold and forewarned by visionaries?

Quick definitions

AR: Augmented Reality: (e.g. *Pokémon Go*) AR adds digital elements to the real world and projects them onto your line of sight. Using AR, workers can view an overlay of 3D models and project information at a job site.

Haptic: Relating to the sense of touch, in particular relating to the perception and manipulation of objects using the senses of touch and proprioception. Haptic feedback devices create the illusion of substance and force within the virtual world.

HMD: Head-mounted display.

MR: Mixed Reality: (e.g. Microsoft® HoloLens®) MR is a hybrid of virtual reality and augmented reality. Using MR, you can touch a real table and use it as an interface to manipulate a digital model.

VR: Virtual Reality: (e.g. Oculus) VR replaces the real world with a simulated one in 3D. With VR, you can experience a simulation of a factory you've designed – with machines running – all before it's built.

XR: See VR/AR/MR.

Types of virtual reality

Game-based VR (e.g. Oculus Rift, Oculus Quest, HTC Vive) and cinematic-based VR (e.g. Oculus Go). Game-based VR utilizes a game engine (like Unreal® or Unity) and has motion tracking so the player can walk around and interact with the environment. Cinematic-based is 360-degree video filmed using a panoramic camera system and played back as an equirectangular video file (rectangular map projection which wraps onto a sphere), which allows the user to look around the scene by turning his/her head but the user cannot walk around or interact with the scene. Depending on the camera system and stitching process, the scenes can be either monoscopic (flat) or stereoscopic (3D).

A moving target

This chapter is less about the history of VR than an effort to collect some important landmarks and to ask meaningful questions while experiencing history being formed. Like Heisenberg's Uncertainty Principle, without the advantage of hindsight, we can only state with accuracy position (what is happening right now) or momentum (trends). We cannot state with certainty an outcome that is based on the combined influences of position and momentum. Borrowing from British science fiction writer Arthur C. Clarke's "Hazards of Prophecy," and his often-cited Third Law, "Any sufficiently advanced technology is indistinguishable from magic," we can loosely redefine modern magic as a technology that has the power to influence us at a visceral or intuitive level and bend or create new realities. The immersive and modified reality capabilities of VR, AR, and MR (XR) have been noted to have more potential psychological and sociological shaping than any medium before. It is perhaps this powerful potential that is causing a faster technological development cycle than we have ever witnessed.

Investors, enterprises, and corporations base many of their organizational directions on Gartner (a global research and advisory firm that publishes an annual "Hype Cycle," "Magic Quadrant," and many other periodic news releases), and this has propelled much of the momentum in XR development. According to Gartner's "Hype Cycle" (2018) virtual reality is no longer an emerging technology but rapidly approaching maturity. Maturity means that the concept or product has passed through four stages (invention, exaggerated expectations, disappointment, and realistic application) to the fifth stage, maturity (production/application to solve real problems).

Regarding AR, in 2019 Gartner predicted that over 100 million consumers would shop using AR in 2020. Retailers such as Ikea, Bob's Discount Furniture, Macy's, Anthropologie, Pottery Barn, Amazon, Alibaba, Sephora, L'Oréal, Sally Hansen, Bella Luce, Lowe's, Home Depot, Sherwin Williams, Gap, Nike, Lacoste, and Converse are using or have plans to use some form of AR to help customers visualize their products during pre-purchase. AR and/or MR in the use of company logistics and procedures is being used (as in smart glasses) for shipping (DHL), AI-driven virtual assistants (VAs) for employees (Amazon, Nokia), and virtual personal assistants (VPAs) as used by Amazon/Marriot. Gartner also predicted that by 2019, 20% of large enterprise businesses would be using XR solutions.

Simply put, XR is becoming, or already is, too big to fail. With billions of dollars invested and some of the largest corporations involved, anyone not involved is afraid of being left behind. With uses far beyond entertainment and including education, medicine, healthcare, fitness, psychology, retail, communications, manufacturing, marketing, design, engineering, and training, everyone can find some solution using XR. Apple CEO Tim Cook stated, "I view AR (augmented reality) like I view the silicon here in my iPhone, it's not a product per se, it's a core technology. But there are things to discover before that technology is good enough for the mainstream." The last core technologies of the 20th century were the computer and smart phones, which were enabled and made more powerful through infrastructures like the Internet, satellites, and artificial intelligence.

Due to the above and piggy-backing on progress that took a century before, in just the first two decades of the new millennium we are seeing fully autonomous vehicles and other devices, the Internet of Bodies (IoB), Internet of Things (IoT), Vehicle to Everything (V2X), social credit algorithms, next generation smart devices, next generation security devices, mimicking chatbots, spoof-caller blocking, smart workplaces, quantum computing (machine learning), neomorphic hardware (deep neural networks), democratized (available to the masses) artificial intelligence, edge computing (the opposite of cloud computing and is local to the user), and affordable VR, AR, and MR devices, which will put potential power into the hands of the public. Having gone from CGI that duplicates reality to bending, modifying, and creating reality, we will look at what some are doing with this power and note what some are warning about it.

Before the millennium

When considering the origins of VR, many historical writings include pan-oramic paintings and stereoscopic images and viewers from the 19th century. Some origins were covered in Chapter 2 of this book involving flight simulators, head-mounted display sets, Ivan Sutherland and Bob Sproull's Sword of Damocles, Jaron Lanier coining the term "virtual reality," the movie *Lawnmower Man*, arcade games, Sega's VR glasses, the game console, PC games, the development of the game engine, and motion tracking. But it is really in the 21st century that computers, CGI, the Internet, and artificial intelligence technology advanced sufficiently and could be integrated to allow virtual reality and its counterparts, AR and MR, to become viable products, mediums, and tools. (Chapter 2 covered some of the technological advances contributing to VR.) Additionally, smartphones with high-density displays, high-quality 3D graphics, and an ever-growing supply of new applications created a generation of affordable and lightweight virtual-reality devices. Google Cardboard (2014) is a very inexpensive head mount for use with a smartphone designed to encourage public innovation.

During the millennium

In 2012 Palmer Luckey produced the Oculus VR developer kits from a $2.4 million Kickstarter campaign. In 2014, Facebook CEO Mark Zuckerberg purchased the Oculus VR for $2.3 billion (cash and shares in Facebook). A public version of the product was released in 2016. Also, in 2014 Samsung partnered with Oculus to develop the Gear VR head-mounted display, which works with a smartphone. Zuckerberg subsequently released the first generation of Oculus products (2017–2018) consisting of the Oculus Rift (needs a gaming PC to run), Oculus Go (stand-alone all-in-one), and Oculus Quest (stand-alone game console).

Oculus Story Studio, a division of Oculus VR, was founded in 2014 by Saschka Unseld (Pixar), Max Planck (Pixar), and producer Edward Saatchi. The purpose of the studio was to support animation and general filmmaking in VR. The studio produced three animated projects: *Lost* (2015), *Henry* (2016), and *Dear Angelica* (2017). However, in 2017 Facebook closed the Oculus Story Studio to shift away from internal content in favor of supporting external content. The open source animation software tool, Quill, was developed by the studio to allow animators to draw in 3D wearing a headset.

Game manufacturers continued to create their own VR headset consoles such as the HTC Vive (2015) by Valve Corporation and Sony's PlayStation VR (2016). In addition to interactive video games, there were sports events. Although VR observation of sports events has not caught on with fans (possibly due to lack of physical mobility) as much as it has with video game players. In 2017 the NBA released the best moments of the year from live games. A partnership between Intel and the NBA created True VR. Using sports channel TNT, True VR is a court-side seat available at the Samsung Gear VR store and the Oculus Go store. Other VR sports channels include Next VR (a collection of sports and other channel content), FOX Sports VR, and ESPN VR. Intel True VR offered 360-degree VR Olympics in 2018 to display 30 different events.

Rather than working on VR 360, Microsoft appears to be focusing on AR and MR, especially in the form of the HoloLens (which overlays graphics on top of the real world). It was announced in 2015, but as of 2019 the pre-order cost of $3,500 limits the consumer base. The concept of using glasses to augment reality with graphics has more appeal to business, science, and enterprise rather than consumer entertainment. It appears Microsoft is trying to build a separate niche market for manipulated reality apart from the consumer market, which may already be glutted. Presently, the technology is open to developers.

Likewise, Google Glass (smart glasses and ubiquitous computer) was released to a select few in 2013 and pulled as a consumer product in 2015 amid privacy invasion accusations (i.e. people fearful that they were being recorded by wearers without permission). There is a second-generation device that will be solely for business use. The cost of $1,500 is better suited for corporations who may use it for their employees to view item data for product development or management.

As a virtual production company, The Third Floor (TTF) is deeply involved in VR so that it can support its clients in creating VR content. *The Martian* movie was released in 2015 (directed by Ridley Scott) and the 25-minute *The Martian VR Experience* (2016, produced by Ridley Scott and directed by Robert Stromberg) immersive 360-degree production debuted at the Las Vegas Consumer Electronics Show to rave reviews and awards. TTF collaborated with the director, Ridley Scott Associates (RSA), and Fox Innovation Lab to create CG assets, developed interactive technology, and optimized platform performance using Epic's Unreal® Engine Version 4.13. *The Martian VR Experience* is available on PlayStation VR, HTC Vive on Steam, or Oculus Rift. In 2016, TTF CEO Chris Edwards was honored with a seat on the BAFTA (British Academy of Film and Television Arts) VR advisory board.

Ridley Scott also founded RSA, the film production company and launched RSA VR in 2017. This division is dedicated to the production of high-end immersive films using VR, AR, and MR. Scott and his associates are known for work on acclaimed films such as *Alien* (1979), *Blade Runner* (1982),

Gladiator (2000), *Black Hawk Down* (2001), and more. RSA was involved in the production of *The Martian VR Experience* (2016) and released *Alien: Covenant In Utero* 360-VR in 2017 with 20th Century Fox. It is available on Steam 360 and Oculus Rift. They are working on two more Alien installments.

In 2018 Steven Spielberg, ILM, Warner Brothers, and Amblin produced the movie *Ready Player One* about the world in 2048 when VR is used to escape a dystopian existence and there is a struggle to own and control the virtual game space, OASIS. The movie has won many awards for visual effects. Based on the bestselling nostalgic book of the same name by Ernest Cline. The movie is notable for its effort to predict how VR will be used in the future and its impact on society (i.e. when VR becomes more real and desirable to us than the physical world).

Much of the effort by VR movie-production entities is to develop storytelling language and strategies for 360 VR. It is debatable whether this medium should use a narrative style at all or just be like live mystery theater in which the audience participates with the actors. These two different approaches are based on the two types of VR (cinematic- and game-based), and depend on the devices used, either a panoramic camera or a game engine.

Game VR is fully immersive and interactive. The player can usually walk around in the environment, pick up objects, receive realistic dimensional sound cues, see portions of the avatar self, and can see other avatars playing the game. Available examples of this are game PCs with HMDs like HTC Vive, Oculus Rift, or Oculus Quest, and the VOID interactive theme park VR game destinations. Storytelling in game VR is based on gameplay with multiple levels (locations), activities, and goals. Game players are an active consumer audience.

Cinematic VR is not fully immersive or interactive. The viewer is stationary but can look around in a 360-degree environment. Viewer movement is controlled by the VR camera. If it moves, the viewer has the sensation of gliding or flying. In this manner, the viewer is captive and so certain types of camera movement may result in the viewer experiencing vertigo-like symptoms. Unlike game VR in which the player is grounded on the floor and autonomous in walking and other movement, cinematic VR controls the viewer by the use of camera movement. This is one of the reasons it has attracted the attention of conventional moviemakers who are experienced in creating entertainment for a passive audience.

The moviemaking process has experienced a substantial disruption during the last century (as was partially covered in Chapter 2 with Figure 2.1 overview) due to electronics and CG, and now, XR. The four main components of moviemaking have traditionally been story, locations/sets, actors, and crew. All four have been drastically changed. In regard to locations and sets, previously there existed stock footage libraries, which stored location film shots used to save time and money when historical period scenes or distant regions were needed in a movie. However, today, the locations, sets, cinematography, and lighting have merged and blurred the separation of these processes into complete virtual production services and systems. Stargate Studios is a one-stop shopping service that offers previsualization, virtual production, and digital library/backlot into a fully integrated turnkey service. It was founded in 1989 by cinematographer, special visual effects supervisor, and producer, Sam Nicholson. Lightcraft Technology is a virtual studio in a box system. Founded in 2004 by Eliot Mack (MIT, Walt Disney Imagineering), the Previzion VFX system is a real-time visual effects system that combines high-precision camera tracking, rendering, and VFX quality keying for use in on-set compositing of virtual backgrounds and CGI characters. Paul Debevec, Senior Scientist at Google VR and Adjunct Research Professor of Computer Science in the Viterbi School of Engineering at the University of Southern California (working within the Vision and Graphics Laboratory at the USC Institute for Creative Technologies), joined Google after they bought Lytro in 2018 and modified their light field camera with a single lens into a camera system with 16 modified GoPro cameras. The result is that realistic light capture containing multiple rays of light from multiple perspectives creates a fully lit environment where the light follows the viewers' eyes no matter where the participant looks within the scene. This means that the viewer can see changing reflections and look around objects. This is basically a lighting and perspective library of data within a scene from multiple viewpoints.

When it comes to CG actors, some advances were covered in Chapter 2. Like digital location and set data, character data too is being collected and stored for repurposing later. The rise of virtual actors (synthespians, virtual stuntmen/women, vactors, cyberstars) can be looked upon as more opportunity for professional actors, a means to resurrect dead actors, or a way to own an actor's persona perpetually without compensation. Motion capture has introduced the "performance actor" or one whose actions and expressions are data kept for immediate or later use. While currently there are not many performance capture actors, the list may grow. It is uncertain how consistent the work may be and how welcoming it will be to new actors.

In Chapter 2 some numbers were presented showing a rise in digital workers but then a drop after technology stabilized. Likewise, the size and roles of traditional movie crews fell in response to and replacement by their digital counterparts. While virtual stuntmen/women may be safer and some dangerous effects, like pyrotechnics and car crashes, might be safer executed in CG, those physical jobs are lost. Certainly, the decentralization of filmmaking caused many in Hollywood to relocate or retrain for other jobs. Virtual production means that production crews need not be so large and efficiency may reduce the need for more post-production people. Then as the technology stabilizes and less new digital assets need to be created, there will then be less need for digital workers, too. The dropping cost of tools, which opens up moviemaking and VR entertainment-making to the masses might involve more people but at a reduced cost, which has the potential for higher profits. It is unclear how virtual production and XR will affect jobs.

Although, the popularity of movie franchises has resulted in the process of creating an immersive fictional universe called "worldbuilding." With the best example of this being The Lord of the Rings franchise, world-building borrows most of its creative and construction process from video game-making. Leaning heavily on sci-fi and fantasy literature as early models of worldbuilding, it has caught the attention of virtual production studios, entrepreneurs, innovators, social disruptors, and universities as a means to redefine communication, art, commerce, society, and possibly the future of mankind. In 2014, the new World Building Media Lab (WBML) opened at the USC Zemeckis Center for Digital Arts. Alex McDowell RDI is the director of WBML and was production designer on *Fear and Loathing in Las Vegas* (1998), *Fight Club* (1999), *Minority Report* (2002), *Charlie and the Chocolate Factory* (2005), *Watchmen* (2009), and *Man of Steel* (2013). An off-shoot of WBML, World Building Institute (WBI) posts international events for worldbuilders, interdisciplinary experts, and storytellers everywhere. A quote from the Berlinale Talents 2019 event stated, "There is no more science fiction. Everything we can imagine will exist, and the power of combining knowledge with imagination will manifest deliberate change, now and in the future." Is this statement a vestige of VR as an emergent technology and exaggerating its potential?

As authors Robert Scoble and Shel Israel explain in *The Fourth Transformation: How Augmented Reality and Artificial Intelligence Will Change Everything* (2016), there were three transformations leading up to XR: using text to talk to computers and the emergence of the personal computer (1970s); the graphical user interface (GUI), which allowed people to talk to computers with clicks and icons (1980s); and using touch screens to talk to your mobile smartphone (2000s). The fourth transformation radically changes how we interact with smart devices by moving away from keyboards, mice, and touchscreens to wearable devices (i.e. glasses and headsets). A wearable device uses more of our senses, is attached to our space, and results in a more experiential interaction with the device, its outcomes, and the other humans we are interacting with.

This is called spatial computing and results in making the world our interface and always online (Scoble and Israel, *The Fourth Transformation*). The three adoption waves of spatial computing evolution that the authors suggest are: 1) virtual reality, 2) mixed reality, and 3) smart glasses.

As a product of multiple other previous technological developments, VR could not exist without them. But because it is an offshoot of the combination of all these technologies, it has a tendency to not follow any of the previous purposes or directions of those technologies and is in the evolutionary process of creating its own direction. Due to its immersive potential, it has the capability of being the most influential communicative tool because it need not rely on only words and pictures (as most communication has done in the past) but communicates swiftly in the realm of experience. The absorption of experiential data that happens during immersion is the illusion of being somewhere you are not physically. However, there is also a blurring of identity. Michael Madary and Thomas Metzinger were part of an investigation to study the philosophical and ethical aspects of VR as part of a five-year research program by the European Commission. The result was a preliminary Code of Ethics published in 2016 (https://www.frontiersin.org/articles/10.3389/frobt.2016.00003/full). They found that virtual reality is inherently different from 2D screen activities because there is no separation between what happens to "my character" and what happens to "me." This was discovered in bias tests involving racism in which a participant would occupy the avatar of a person of a different race. It was also found that psychological effects of VR experience could be long-lasting. In the service of good, this could mean better medical treatment, and some have touted VR as an empathy machine. ("Empathy machine" came out of a 2015 TED Talk by artist, entrepreneur, and director Chris Milk based on his collaboration with the United Nations on the VR film, *Clouds Over Sidra* (2015), which is a look inside the life of Sidra, a 12-year-old Syrian refugee.) Currently there are ongoing multiple research and reviews regarding VR and empathy with one of the most publicized ones being The Machine to Be Another (see http://beanotherlab.org/home/work/tmtba/), which is an open source artistic body-swapping experiment, and Project Empathy. These experiments are based on brain cells called mirror neurons, which activate when a person performs an action and when a person observes another performing the same action. In this way, a person can feel what an action is like. Aside from definitions and being aware of differences between sympathy, empathy, and compassion, results are inconclusive, yet study into shaping human attitudes and influencing society persist. "VR can create deep emotional connections in a very short period of time." Glen Gilmore, Principal at the social media marketing firm Gilmore Business Network, said to consider its "'hyper-social' effects" (https://medium.com/@glengilmore/24-takeaways-from-the-fourth-transformation-472854170843).

A review of VR research by the US National Library of Medicine, National Institutes of Health (NIH) concluded virtual environments that promote positive stimuli and are used with medical knowledge could be valuable for public and mental health. Among the more promising uses were pain and stress management, with treatment for more serious conditions such as anxieties, phobias, addiction, and PTSD (Post Traumatic Stress Disorder) requiring more research. The reduced cost of head-mounted displays (HMDs) increases public access to such therapies.

China may well lead the way in remote VR education. Because of their immense population, they cannot train teachers fast enough so technology is being used to create virtual teachers and classrooms. As of a 2018 article, the company Judao has promised to use VR for all the schools in China within three years. Although VR is more expensive than traditional teaching, they believe that it results in a better education and are adding AR into instruction also. Regarding virtual teachers, students can change the gender, teaching speed, and other instructional options to customize their education. In the US, VR is being used for field trips, instructional content, and there is still much discussion surrounding remote classrooms for school safety.

The authors of *The Fourth Transformation* warn that allowing governments and avatars to have too much control and influence over us all may result in further division and disconnect between humans in social communication. Would we look up to AI avatars instead of to each other? Would we use the technology to escape and avoid compassion or controversial issues? Would we be over-marketed and data-mined to death? What about social credit system abuses (a form of mass surveillance using big data analysis affecting individual reputation, which is something that China started experiencing in 2018). Another result of the Michael Madary and Thomas Metzinger Code of Ethics research is that "The power of V.R. to induce particular kinds of emotions could be used deliberately to cause suffering. Conceivably, the suffering could be so extreme as to be considered torture." Should restrictions be placed on XR content in general and horror movies in particular? The latest trend in movies is excessive violence and sex. Because of immersive reality's visceral and long-lasting effects, should some form of censorship be reintroduced to entertainment material? In the service of malice, virtual devices create another hackable portal opportunity. What type of security and privacy protections should be used?

Still, with more stand-alone HMDs, reduction in costs, content that has longevity, continuing creation of new applications, innovative uses that were not considered in the past because there are more developers on board now, more automated devices, and more consumers/buyers willing to pay for content,

XR is, again, too big to fail. Most importantly, the advanced ability for communication and collaboration cannot be underemphasized. With transportation becoming more expensive and even more dangerous, the ability to collaborate together worldwide yet feel as if everyone is in the same space is a game changer. If AI can provide a virtual assistant, automatic speech translation, meeting recordings, and avatars with realistic facial expressions, and MR/AR can provide white boards, 3D object interaction, the ability to work across platforms and a big display screen, then groups can work together. Again, there is a Chinese company, VR Waibao, working on this. In 2018, the Chinese government released a document about their commitment to XR and wants to be a world leader. As Mark Zuckerberg said about the acquisition of Oculus VR, "This is really a new communication platform." There is a worldwide race to dominate this new medium.

However, outside of commerce there are some who are examining XR's potential influence on social consciousness and enlightenment. If IoT (the Internet of Things), Vehicle to Everything (V2X), and potentially IoB (the Internet of Body) is the nervous system of the fourth transformation, then AI is its soul. AI autonomous decision-making is based on collection of massive data from human voice pattern recognition, human visual recognition, human tasks execution, and human choices filtered through secret algorithms for secret intentions and purposes created by humans to control and manipulate other humans. Stories like Steven Spielberg's *A.I. Artificial Intelligence* (2001) pose questions that remind us how very little we know about human consciousness and what motivates us.

Not knowing what consciousness is makes it difficult to write algorithms and systems that accurately imitate us. An article in *Science* magazine published in 2017, "What is consciousness, and could machines have it?" defined three types of consciousness: C0 calculations that happen outside of our attention (e.g. facial pattern recognition), C1 evaluating global data to make circumstantial deliberate choices, and C2 self-monitoring or meta-cognition to correct our own mistakes and explore the unknown.

What does this have to do with XR? Every new medium extends our bodies and consciousness a little bit more. Each new medium becomes an extension of ourselves and can transform us (Marshall McLuhan, *Understanding Media: The Extensions of Man*, 1964). McLuhan also coined the phrase "the medium is the message" meaning that the channel of transmission is more important than the content. Since we are often blind to a pervasive medium that has become invisible through constant use, we focus on the content and miss how we have been altered by the medium. One example is movies, which altered linear time and speed through photography and editing. It changed our perception of reality to configurations. Likewise, XR's immersion, layering of graphic and real elements, and body shifting to avatars can alter perceptions of time, space, speed, and identity.

Easy adaptation to each new medium makes us blind to the medium itself resulting in a condition McLuhan called "narcissus narcosis," which is a "peculiar form of self-hypnosis." Although he died in 1980, his description of this condition is seen today in overuse of cell phone "selfies," which has gained much public attention through the increase of accidents and falls, to a growing form of body dysmorphic disorder labeled "Snapchat dysmorphia," which has been noted by cosmetic surgeons. This new generation of younger patients want to look like their filtered images on Snapchat, which are so exaggerated as to be unobtainable. Overuse of social media has made a generation of people obsessed with their public image and mixing realistic facial/body features with fantasy.

If there is not a widespread accepted definition of consciousness, there is also no definition of reality. Hyper-reality is defined by two main concepts, simulation and simulacra in a book written by Jean Baudrillard (*Simulacra and Simulation*, 1981). Simulacra is the concept that our lives are constructed of symbols and signs shaped by culture and media and constitute what passes for reality. True simulacra is reached by a gradual deviance from physical reality in which stage one is a faithful copy of reality, stage two is an unfaithful copy, stage three (the "order of sorcery") pretends to be a faithful copy but is actually an original, and stage four is when the simulacrum has no relationship to reality at all. Simulation is a blending of physical reality and representation, much like a map is a representation of geography. Simulation does not exist in a physical realm but in a space without boundaries. In this sense, the map has become or superseded the territory. Together simulacra and simulation constitute hyper-reality. Baudrillard uses Los Angeles and Disneyland as examples of hyper-reality (and one might also suggest Las Vegas). We can also see examples of this in modern moviemaking and storytelling such as *300* (2006) in which the history of the Battle of Thermopylae within the Persian Wars is rewritten.

XR is the latest hyper-reality medium or combination of mediums. In 2016, the first of the VOID (Visions of Infinite Dimensions, VR theme park) franchise locations opened in Pleasant Grove, Utah, with others to follow in London, Dubai, Toronto, Atlanta, Austin, Dallas, Orlando, Minneapolis, New York, Philadelphia, Washington, D.C., Anaheim, Glendale, Santa Monica, Hollywood, Edmonton, Mississauga, and Las Vegas. The VOID was founded by CEO Ken Bretschneider, Curtis Hickman (a visual effects artist and former stage magician), and James M. Jensen (an entrepreneur and interactive media designer). The themes and partnerships include the themes and studios such as Ghostbusters (Sony Pictures) and Star Wars, Ralph Breaks the Internet, and

Marvel (Disney). (Meanwhile Walt Disney World Resort in Florida opened a physical attraction, Star Wars: Galaxy's Edge in 2019.) The technology of their virtual reality includes physical effects; head-mounted display helmet: noise-canceling headphones; hand-tracking sensor; a haptic suit containing 22 vibrators; and a computer to power the headset. Players freely walk through and explore a virtual world while in a stage equipped with ceiling-mounted motion tracking cameras to read the users' movements. To provide physical feedback, the stage contains foam walls, special effects equipment such as fans, mist machines, and heat lamps, as well as props representing items such as guns and torches. All of these physical elements interact with elements within the virtual world seen through the headset, thereby completing the illusion of immersion. Its website promises "The VOID creates real memories in a virtual world."

Steve Mann is the author of the book *Cyborg: Digital Destiny and Human Possibility in the Age of the Wearable Computer* (2001) and pioneer of wearable devices to extend his powers of perception such as a miniature head-mounted display in glasses, on-board networked computing, and recording devices. He asks,

> How will we post-humans grapple with the awesome powers to reinvent humanity and society that technology has bestowed on us? To what extent are individuals free to alter their own bodies and minds? To what extent will individual mind/body alterations affect other members of society?

He reminds us that many of these developments were products of military research and were not made for distraction but have sobering and serious applications.

Having experienced, participated, and survived the first three transformations including the changes to moviemaking in the latter 20th century, there are some aspects that are repeating but many others that are new. Therefore, the fourth transformation is more difficult to predict and respond to. Isaac Asimov said, "The saddest aspect of life right now is that science gathers knowledge faster than society gathers wisdom." The repetition of fast-moving technology that is at first chaotic due to so many different viewpoints surrounding the change in addition to some areas of resistance, appears to be a common condition of new technology. This presents a challenge to adaption and adoption. What is different about today's metaverse (today defined as a combination of Internet, AI, and XR, originally coined by Neal Stephenson, 1992, in his science fiction novel *Snow Crash*) is the amazing swiftness of integration and public release of systems, tools, and applications whose results cannot be accurately predicted. The pattern appears to follow stages of concept, production, release, then analysis. This leaves us all open to negative results that could be very difficult to reverse once in widespread use. Technology hides intentions which can be difficult to read. Using technology to diminish or exploit others can result in perpetual conflict. For example, a subscription-based economy without safeguards to income could result in selective poverty. Secret algorithms and automated decision-making could result in covert societal/political/financial manipulation. British science fiction writer Arthur C. Clarke devised three dictums that are known as Clarke's Three Laws, of which the Third Law is the best known and most widely quoted, "Any sufficiently advanced technology is indistinguishable from magic." A popular variant of this Third Law by an unknown author is, "Any sufficiently advanced cluelessness is indistinguishable from malice." While a bit pessimistic, cluelessness abounds during the chaotic period of new technology. However, cluelessness can be addressed with education thereby eliminating some accidental malice. In a more optimistic vein, we all adapt so quickly and easily to any convenience we forget what life was like without it. The advantages may well outweigh the risks. As Arthur C. Clarke stated in his Second Law, "The only way of discovering the limits of the possible is to venture a little way past them into the impossible." A certain amount of research, risk-taking, and optimism is important if we are to grow and thrive.

Poet William Butler Yeats once wrote, "The visible world is no longer a reality and the unseen world is no longer a dream." We have truly entered a period in mankind's history of miracles and magic in which we have set out on paths that take us far away from our origins. So, what will you do? The following ideas presented for reflection are loosely based on this author's review of "Real virtuality: a code of ethical conduct. Recommendations for good scientific practice and the consumers of VR-technology" by Michael Madary and Thomas K. Metzinger (2016) and a review of "Career advice I wish I'd been given when I was young" by an anonymous author (2019).

1. Do no harm. Experiment ethically, talk about the risks of XR, and get informed consent.
2. Solve problems that aren't popular. Not only will your competition be less but you may find yourself to be an early expert and this may help you figure out how to brand yourself.
3. Read a lot, especially history. Aside from the continual technical information out there, find topics that others may not know about.
4. Crowdsource ideas. Network and find people you like and respect and discuss some of your most useful ideas.
5. Focus on interesting projects instead of just taking jobs that pay the bills. Prioritize wisely and use your time and effort where it will serve you best.
6. Don't promise false hope. Give people the facts and let them make up their own minds.

7. Be aware of dual use. Much of XR has good and bad purposes. For example, VR can be used to encourage compassion, but it can also be used to elicit hatred. Know the ways your application can be used not just how you want it to be used.

8. Be aware of Internet and AI dual use. The Internet and AI have good and bad purposes and XR media may compound that. Know the ways that others will use your application remotely and in automated decision-making.

9. Be aware of public risk to long-term immersion, lack of control, or autonomy over an avatar or situation, dangerous environments or simulations, and privacy breach.

10. Take care of yourself. Mind your physical and mental health. Look for activities and projects that you enjoy. Make friends. Be mindful of your reputation.

The torch has been passed. Carry it well.

About the authors

Baby pictures

After graduating from USC (USC School of Cinema-Television, later changed to USC School of Cinematic Arts in 2006), Juniko began working at Roger Corman's New World studio at the dawn of the motion-control era. From there she worked on a number of feature projects including as a motion-control operator at ILM for the film *Innerspace* (1987). Moody transitioned to computer graphics while working for the Ultimatte Corporation as a product specialist. Her experience with SGI (Silicon Graphics, Inc.) and TDI (Thomson

Digital Image) hardware and software led her to work with the Eastman Kodak Corporation division of Cinesite, Los Angeles, on the digital restoration of Disney's animated movie *Snow White* (originally released 1937, restored 1993). Following that project led her to work for Warner Brothers, Sony, and Walt Disney Feature Animation for the film *Dinosaur* (2000) in the role of CGI lighting and digital compositing. She transitioned to corporate training for Dreamworks and then stepped away from production to share her knowledge by teaching at several colleges. Continuing to work in academia she graduated from USC Rossier School of Education with a Doctor of Education degree. She has authored the science-fiction book, *The Button Chronicles* (2015), that is being represented by Marasco Management for development into a television series.

Mark began as a high-school clay animation hobbyist when he enrolled at USC School of Cinema-Television. He co-produced and did effects work on the low budget feature *The Strangeness* (1985) that led him to work at Roger Corman's New World Pictures/New Horizons studio. After several features he became the lead optical cameraman for CMI, winning a Clio award for his commercial work. This experience led him to be hired by Illusion Arts as the lead matte cameraman working under Bill Taylor, shooting classic matte paintings by Albert Whitlock, Syd Dutton, and Robert Stromberg. The next leg of the journey was to be co-VFX supervisor for Area 51 on the Emmy-winning Tom Hanks' project "From the Earth to the Moon" (1998). He then went on to become the head cameraman for Custom Film Effects creating VFX and opticals for many feature films. Throughout his career, Mark shared his knowledge as an author and educator and taught at several colleges and schools such as The Stan Winston School of Character Arts and the Global Cinematography Institute. He is currently developing television content based on his *Filming the Fantastic* books and continues to work on independent projects as a consultant and actor.

Index

Page references in *italics* indicate an illustration.